Easy Food Dehydrating and Safe Food Storage

Susan Gast

DEDICATION

I'd like to dedicate this book to all who believe in preparing
for the unknown, not in a blind panic, but in an orderly fashion.

I'd also like to dedicate this book to all of the Facebook fans
and loyal readers who took the time to post, and send
in comments via our "Contact Us" form on our website:
www.easy-food-dehydrating.com

Thank You.

CONTENTS

ACKNOWLEDGMENTS

"Things happen when they're supposed to."
My dad always manages to send the appropriate email
at just the right time that spurs me into action.
I don't know how he knows, but he does!

A big "thanks" to my husband, Alan, who has tolerated
many evenings of late-night typing and editing.
His patience and understanding is very much appreciated.

And to my "mum" – who always asks me daily
"How are you doing?"

~*~

1
WELCOME!

Allow Easy Food Dehydrating to show you just how easy it is to prepare and create dehydrated food — no more worries about throwing away spoiled foods — dehydrate it, store it — and you're good to go — anytime of the year!

follow our
simple steps
to dehydrate food safely

We'll show you how to make dehydrated fruit, dehydrated vegetables, and dehydrated meats... along with some dehydrated pet treats!

We also have tips on how to store your dehydrated foods for long-term food storage, so you can beat inflation, and a possible food shortage caused by changing weather patterns and/or inflation.

Long-term food storage is on the minds of many people. It's now more important than ever to have long-term food supplies on hand, due to inflation wreaking havoc on food prices at our grocery stores!

While you're here, check out our food dehydrator and food vacuum sealer info. -- it's how you get the food from the grocery store, or garden, into your bags, bins, buckets, and jars!

Don't forget to check out our free dehydrated food recipes!

Now it's time to get started! We're very happy that you have this book to show you how to prepare for food shortages and save money by dehydrating your fresh produce (or frozen food from the stores) in the comfort of your own home so you can create easy meals at the drop of a hat with our free recipes!

Before we get going, there's something I wish to add here, which is from feedback I received regarding the Kindle version of this book. The reader found the use of "Don't forget to rotate your trays for even drying" a bit repetitious but she did say she understood the need for it. This is how I see it: Some people will buy this book purely to find out how to dehydrate, let's say, "tomatoes" and "apples" and not look at anything else. If I only mentioned once to "rotate your trays" in the beginning of the book, I risk you not seeing that important comment at all – therefore you'll see it in every fruit and vegetables "how-to" instructions. I did appreciate the feedback from the Kindle book purchaser, and want to "apologize" in advance to you if you find some parts "repetitious" – *now you know why!*

Thanks for reading this and we hope you'll enjoy this book and will also leave us some feedback in the comments section at Amazon.com.

2
DISCLAIMER

Easy Food Dehydrating provides this book as a service.

The information contained within the book is no guarantee that the information provided in this book is correct, complete, and/or up-to-date. You use the information at your own risk.

The materials contained in this book are provided for general information purposes only and do not constitute legal or other professional advice on any subject matter.

Easy Food Dehydrating does not accept any responsibility for any loss which may arise from reliance on information contained on this book.

The contents of this book are protected by copyright under international conventions and, apart from your purchase, the reproduction, permanent storage, or retransmission of the contents of this book is prohibited without the prior written consent of Easy Food Dehydrating.

Some links within this book may lead to other websites, including those operated and maintained by third parties. Easy Food Dehydrating includes these links solely as a convenience to you, and the presence of such a link does not imply a responsibility for the linked site or an endorsement of the linked site, its operator, or its contents (exceptions may apply).

3
HOW TO DEHYDRATE FRUIT, VEGETABLES, AND MEAT

Our easy-to-follow instructions show you how to safely dehydrate fresh or frozen food, so you'll have it in your pantry to use for weeks and months, instead of just for a few days, before it spoils!

No More Money Wasted
Throwing Out Spoiled Food!
Beat Soaring Food Prices
Save Money Now – Dehydrate Food at Today's Prices!

When fully re-hydrated, Dehydrated Food looks and tastes the same as it did in its fresh state and is fantastic for whipping up soups and stews. It's also great for long-term food storage -- we'll show you how to safely store all your goodies too, away from air, moisture, bugs… and prying eyes!

4
SIX SIMPLE STEPS

The basis of the first simple step is to buy foods that are on sale or in season! Buy Fresh Produce OR Frozen from the grocery store freezers! Maybe it's time to start growing your own fruits and vegetables too. Consider buying fresh foods in bulk. Visit local farms, and stop by those fantastic road-side fruit and vegetable stands. Get to know your local farmers!

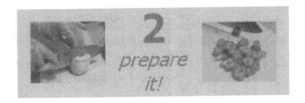

Preparing your food is step number two - simply by washing, blanching, steaming, or spraying with lemon juice! The lemon juice deters oxidation so the food doesn't go brown. If you go the easiest route with frozen foods, there's no preparation involved - now that's easy!

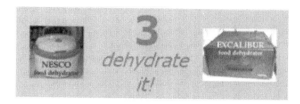

Step Three: Dehydrate your foods by using an electric dehydrator, and read a brief overview on the main fruit and vegetable pages. Then simply select the fruit of your choice, or a vegetable you like! There's even a section on cooked meats for easy-to-do dehydration at home too!

Step Four: Condition your foods - Place cooled foods into air tight bags, such as zip-lock bags, so that the air and moisture in the bag circulates and distributes evenly! Let them sit out on your counter-top for a day or overnight.

Simple step five consists of vacuuming the air out of your bags. Place your food in the vacuum sealer bag with an oxygen pack. We are now ready to use a vacuum sealer machine to draw the air out of the bags -- this is a lot of fun!

Step six is the final step in our journey of dehydrating food and storing it away in a safe place. Store your foods in Mylar bags, and finally in plastic lidded bins or feed buckets with lids -- for the long-term.

5
YOUR DEHYDRATING FRUIT HQ

Enjoy the Fruits of Your Labor – even in the off-season!

The best time for dehydrating fruit is at the peak of season when your favorite fruits are readily available... you'll save money too. You can have dried apples, oranges, and strawberries available TO YOU year 'round now!

Yummy healthy snacks... and dare I mention great baked apple pies!! So make a quick trip to your local grocery store, on even better, to those great road-side stands and buy your apples by the bushel! Visit a local orchard if one is close by.

Dehydrated apples, bananas, and strawberries can be in your family's backpacks, lunch bags - and your pantry. Create tasty fruit rolls -- it's nature's own candy -- and your kids will love them! They are fantastic for backpacking snacks too!

Pick a Fruit

APPLES

APRICOTS

BANANAS

BERRIES

CHERRIES

FRUIT ROLLS

GRAPES

LEMONS, LIMES, ORANGES

MELONS

PEACHES

PEARS

PLUMS

RHUBARB

STRAWBERRIES

How Much Fruit Should I Buy To Fill 4 Dehydrator Trays?

An Easy Guide For Fruit

Most of us do not have tons of spare room in our fridges and freezers, so before you go out buying too much, here's a handy guide that shows how much fruit will fit on four dehydrator trays. Please remember this is just a guide. It's not an exact science...

FRUIT

Apples: fresh, 3-4 medium

Apricots: fresh, 5 whole per tray (20 total); frozen, 2lb bag

Bananas: fresh, 6-8 medium to large

Berries: fresh or frozen, 2lb

Cherries: fresh or frozen, 2lb

Grapes: fresh, 1lb if cut in half; 2lb if left whole

Citrus: 4-5 medium oranges, 7-8 lemons or limes

Melon: 2lbs diced

Peaches: fresh, 4 whole if slicing; 16 whole if halving - but please note: you may have to use an Excalibur machine which has the ability to remove alternate trays to allow for the height of the peach, so that would drop the quantity down to 8 and two trays; frozen, 2lb

Pears: fresh, 4-6 whole pears; frozen, 2lb

Plums: fresh, 24-28 whole, sliced in half - but please note: you may have to use an Excalibur machine which has the ability to remove alternate trays to allow for the height of the plums, so that would drop the quantity down to 12-14 and two trays; frozen, 2lb
Rhubarb: fresh, 2lbs sliced into 1" chunks
Strawberries: fresh, 1-1/2 to 2lbs; frozen, 2lbs

What's The Ideal Temperature to use for Dehydrating Fruit?

Fruits are best dehydrated between 125°F and 135°F — any hotter than that may cause the skins of certain fruits to get crusty i.e. 'hard'. This is known as 'case hardening' which prevents the inside of the fruit from drying out properly. Don't be tempted to turn the food dehydrator on high to speed up the process!

Preparation for Dehydrating Fruit

Fresh lemons, limes, and oranges can be washed and sliced and put on your food dehydrator with no further preparation necessary!
Select a fruit you wish to dehydrate from the list a few pages back. Each fruit has full dehydrating instructions, specific to your fruit selection.

All frozen fruits can be placed on your dehydrator trays with no further preparation - how easy is that? Before opening your bag of frozen fruit, throw it down onto your counter top (not too hard!) a few times to loosen any fruit that may have frozen together in a clump! If you still have a few small clumps on your dehydrator tray, run it under cold water for a few seconds, not too long under the tap, and that'll take care of the large clumps.

Certain fruits such as bananas, apples, and strawberries, need to have a generous spraying of lemon juice.

Lemon juice is a totally acceptable substitute for ascorbic acid which is used by professional dehydrating plants, and the lemon juice works wonderfully!

There are two reasons for spraying with lemon juice

    1)   prevent the fruits from darkening

    2)   prevents bacterial growth during drying

Dehydrated Fruit is Dry when...

...they don't stick together! Dehydrated fruits such as oranges, lemons, and limes get really dry, almost brittle. Place the fruit in airtight bags, (such as zip-lock bags), and let them hang around your kitchen for a day or overnight.

This is known as conditioning (more on this on pg 134) and this enables the air and any moisture in the bag to distribute evenly – so that the dehydrated fruit will be ready for vacuum sealing! Bear in mind, that some fruits will remain naturally sticky such as prunes, and raisins.

6
DEHYDRATING APPLES

Now then, how 'bout them apples? ...

By dehydrating apples from the grocery store, you can now have a steady supply of apples available to you all year - if you're not lucky enough to have your own apple orchard out back!

This is easily achieved by dehydrating apples at home when they are in season and plentiful via the grocery store in bags or from your own back yard in bushels!

Apple's best vitamins are: vitamin A, vitamin C, followed by vitamin K with trace amounts of Choline, Pantothenic Acid, and Niacin.

The minerals found in apples are Potassium, followed by Phosphorus, Calcium, Magnesium, and trace amounts of Zinc. Apples also contain Omega-3 and Omega-6 fatty acids.

How To Dehydrate Apples

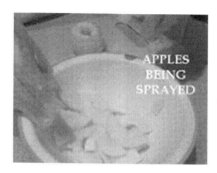

If using frozen apples, ignore steps 1 and 2.

1) Peel, core, and slice your apples with a handy apple-peeler-corer gadget.

2) Place slices in a bowl and generously spray with lemon juice. TIP: Use a pump-top from a new unused spray bottle, pick one that fits your lemon juice bottle, look for one that has a long enough plastic tube that'll reach to the bottom of your lemon juice bottle.

3) Arrange the apple slices on your dehydrator trays, making sure the apples don't overlap.

4) Turn on your food dehydrator and set the temperature between 125°F and 135°F (or per your food dehydrator's instructions).

Delicious dried apples are pliable when dried.

Drying time: between 4-10 hours.

Please remember to rotate your dehydrator trays for even drying.

Simply add water to your dried apples to re-hydrate them, and we're off making the best apple pies around... or applesauce, or apple breads, or cookies...

You'll want one of those apple-peeler-corer gadgets as shown in the first photo... Honest! Not only are they easy to use, they are truly fascinating to watch! Go to Amazon and get yours today. (You can also peel potatoes with them!)

Mmmm-mmm... Soon the delicious apple-pie aroma from your kitchen will be drawing friends and neighbors for miles!

This photo shows three vacuum-sealed bags of dehydrated apples. More to come on the blue packets – they are Oxygen Absorbers!

7
DEHYDRATING APRICOTS

By dehydrating apricots when they are plentiful, you can have delicious apricot jam, apricot compote, pies, sauces... on hand, year 'round'.

Apricots have a lovely velvety skin and are a fantastic source of vitamin A, followed by vitamin C, and vitamin E, with trace amounts of Folate, Choline, vitamin K, Niacin and vitamin B6.

Apricots contain these minerals: Potassium, Phosphorus, Calcium, and Magnesium, with trace amounts of Iron, Zinc, Selenium, Copper and Manganese.

Apricots also have Omega-6 fatty acids.

Thankfully they are readily available frozen, if you're not lucky enough to have peach trees in your garden -- so this is the easy way to create your own private stock of dehydrated apricots!

How to Dehydrate Apricots

If using frozen apricots, ignore steps 1, 2 and 3.

1) First, prepare your fresh apricots by washing them, cut them in half, and remove the pits.

2) Next we will syrup-blanch the apricots by preparing a mixture of one cup of sugar, 1 cup of white corn syrup, and 2 cups of water. Bring it to a boil then add no more than 2 pounds of prepared fruit to the pan and simmer gently for around 10 minutes.

3) Let them cool in the syrup in the pan, for a good half hour. Lightly rinse with clean cold water.

4) Arrange the apricots on your dehydrator trays, making sure they don't overlap. If you are using an Excalibur dehydrator, you may wish to leave out alternating trays if you find that your apricot halves are too cramped in-between the trays. I find the Nesco dehydrator better suited for dehydrating apricots due to the spacing between their trays.

5) Turn on your food dehydrator and set the temperature between 125°F and 135°F (or per your food dehydrator's instructions).

Apricots are pliable when dried.

Drying time: between 8-16 hours.

To make sure that your dehydrated apricots are indeed dry, take a piece and cut it. The apricot will be pliable still, but no juice should ooze out when squeezed. Please remember to rotate your trays, for even drying.

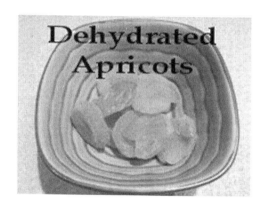

As a kid my family and I vacationed quite a few times in the South of France (lucky me), and my favorite time of day was breakfast! I'd set off on foot in the warm sunshine, clear blue sky overhead... the aroma of freshly-baked bread permeating the air! After getting back from the Patisserie with a huge bag of warm fresh buttery croissants, I could hardly wait to spread on the apricot jam... absolute heaven!

8
DEHYDRATING BANANAS

Dehydrating bananas is quick and makes great banana chips for on-the-go munching. When re-hydrated: voila! Banana Pudding!

Dehydrating bananas is a great way to use up bananas as we all know they tend to turn brown so fast! Bananas are a good source of vitamin A, Choline, vitamin C, vitamin K with trace amounts of Niacin, vitamin B6, Pantothenic Acid, Riboflavin, Betaine, and Thiamin.

Minerally speaking, bananas are loaded with Potassium, followed by Magnesium, Phosphorus, and Calcium. There's trace amounts of Fluoride, Selenium, Manganese, Iron, Zinc and Copper. Bananas contain Omega-3 and Omega-6 fatty acids too.

How to Dehydrate Bananas

1) First, prepare your bananas by unzipping them and slicing evenly. Not too thick and not too thin.

2) You can either use your knife and a chopping board, or use a mandoline. TIP: Chill bananas a short while first for easier slicing – less mushiness!

3) Grab a bowl and generously spray the banana slices with lemon juice, tossing gently to make sure they are evenly coated. TIP: Use a pump-top from a new unused spray bottle, pick one that fits your lemon juice bottle, look for one that has a long enough plastic tube that'll reach to the bottom of your lemon juice bottle.

4) Arrange the sliced bananas on your dehydrator trays, making sure they don't overlap.

5) Turn on your dehydrator and set the temperature between 125°F and 135°F (or per your food dehydrator's instructions).

Dried bananas will feel leathery when fully dried.

Drying time: between 6-12 hours.

Please remember to rotate your trays, for even drying.

Bananas are great any way you slice 'em, but dehydrated bananas are fantastic in granola, banana bread, pudding, cookies... and baby food. Take them along with you on your next outing!

9
DEHYDRATING BERRIES

Dehydrating Blueberries and Cranberries take a little more preparation, but it's well worth the time and effort! You can enjoy dehydrated blueberries and cranberries year 'round!

Blueberries are wonderful sources of vitamin A, vitamin C, followed by vitamin K. Blueberries have trace amounts of Folate, Choline, Niacin, Vitamin E, Betaine, Thiamin, and Riboflavin. The minerals in blueberries are: Phosphorus, Magnesium, and Calcium, with trace amounts of Manganese, Iron, Zinc, and Copper. Blueberries contain Omega-3 and Omega-6 fatty acids too.

And how about a beautiful blueberry pie -- and dress up plain old cereal in the morning! Many of us use cranberries at Christmas time, I mean, what turkey dinner is complete without Cranberry sauce? Cranberries are also a good source of vitamins A, and vitamin C, followed by vitamin K, and Choline, plus trace amounts of Vitamin E, Folate, Pantothenic Acid and Betaine.

The minerals in cranberries are Potassium, Phosphorus, Calcium and Magnesium, with trace amounts of Manganese, Iron, Selenium, Zinc, and copper. Cranberries contain Omega-3 and Omega-6 fatty acids too.

How To Dehydrate Berries

If using frozen berries, ignore steps 1 and 2

1) Prepare your blueberries or cranberries by rinsing them in a sieve, and remove the stems.

2) Dip the berries into boiling water until you see their skins crack! This helps in the dehydrating process.

3) Arrange the blueberries or cranberries on your food dehydrator trays, making sure they don't touch each other so that air can circulate.

4) Turn on your dehydrator and set the temperature between 125°F and 135°F (or per your food dehydrator's instructions).

Dehydrated blueberries and cranberries are leathery when dried.

Drying time: between 10-18 hours.

Remember to rotate your food dehydrator trays, for even drying.

And that reminds me, my mom makes a killer dessert pie using cranberries and pineapple — see Desserts for Mom's Cranberry and Pineapple Pie, see page 258.

10
DEHYDRATING CHERRIES

Dehydrating cherries is a good idea as they are a pretty expensive fruit to buy, so while they're in season, get busy dehydrating this nutritional fruit!

I remember as a kid eating mom's glace cherries which are also known as candied cherries, (trust kids to want to only eat fruit with sugar on or in it, sigh), I used to go to the fridge and sneak a few from the container... I wonder if she ever noticed? :-)

Sour red cherries are packed with vitamin A but are no match for sweet red cherries in the vitamin A department! Sour cherries also have more vitamin C, and Folate.

In the mineral department, cherries are pretty evenly matched: Both sweet and sour red cherries have a great amount of Potassium, followed by a good amount of Phosphorus, Calcium, Magnesium, and have trace amounts of Iron, Zinc, Copper, and Manganese. Both sweet and sour red cherries contain Omega-3 and Omega-6 fatty acids.

They are a versatile fruit: Cherry Cobblers, Cherry Pies, Cherry Toppings, and are used in Fruit Cocktails!

How To Dehydrate Cherries

If using frozen cherries, ignore step one

1) Wash the cherries and remove the stems and pits.

2) Cut in half and place them on your food dehydrator trays with the cut-side up to prevent drips on the lower trays!

3) Turn on your dehydrator and set the temperature between 125°F and 135°F (or per your food dehydrator's instructions).

Drying time: between 18-26 hours and they will feel sticky and leathery when dried.

Make sure you don't over-dry cherries!

Remember to rotate your food dehydrator trays, for even drying.

11
DEHYDRATING FRUIT ROLLS

apple and pear fruit roll mix
in the blender

By dehydrating puréed fruit, you'll create nutritious snacks for your family which are healthy for young and old alike. Dehydrated fruit rolls, (also known as Fruit Leathers, and Fruit Roll-ups - no, not those candies!), are very easy to make and cost less than fruit leathers bought in any store!

Fruit leathers can be made from fresh fruits or any leftover fruits and can be sweetened if desired -- add cinnamon to an apple and pear mix! Yummy!

Add a Little Sweetness!

For added sweetness for fruit rolls when using tart fruits: for each quart of purée add one or two tablespoons of honey or corn syrup -- whichever is on hand in your pantry -- and taste-test 'til your taste-buds are happy! Note: adding regular sugar to fruit rolls can make them become brittle when in storage.

Select a fruit combination for a fruit leather that will appeal to you and your kids! For example bananas and pineapples make a great combination. How about strawberries with rhubarb, or pineapple and cranberry?

Use Fresh Fruit in Season

It's always best to use fresh fruit for your fruit rolls while it's in season and plentiful – read: cheaper – but don't forget you can also use overripe fruits or those misshapen, bruised fruits that didn't quite make it to your fruit bowl on the dining table ... :-(

Canned Fruits

In a pinch? You can use canned fruits too. Simply drain off the excess liquid first (in a sieve, in the sink) then put the fruit in the blender and away you go.

Frozen Fruits are Fabulous Too!

You can even use frozen fruits but be aware that these may be a little thinner in consistency after puréeing. To combat a too runny consistency, let the frozen fruit come to room temperature first, allowing excess water/juice to drain off naturally (in the sink, in a sieve). If it's still too runny, add an apple to the mix!

Use Fruit Roll Sheets or Plastic Wrap

The fruit rolls are easily made by puréeing the fruit in your blender and by spreading it thinly onto your food dehydrator's special sheets created just for this purpose. If you're not using the Nesco fruit-roll sheets, simply lay a sheet of plastic wrap over the trays to make your own drip-proof sheets!

IMPORTANT!

NOTE: DO NOT leave the center hole covered! Cut out the center of the plastic wrap so the air can circulate!

When spreading out the puréed fruit make sure that the center portion of the tray contents is a little thinner than the outer edges, as the outer edges tend to dry out faster. See next photo.

NOTE: When using two Nesco dehydrator fruit roll trays, two large apples and 4 pears were used; this is to give you a rough idea as to how much fruit to use for two sheets.

I also added extra an extra dehydrator tray in-between the two fruit roll trays for added air circulation: Nesco recommends using NO LESS than four trays at a time for proper air circulation.

How To Dehydrate Fruit Rolls

1) Wash your favorite combination of fresh fruit and trim away any bruised and/or spoiled areas.

2) You can leave the skin on -- chop the fruits into 1" chunks to make it easier on your blender and discard the core and seeds.

3) Add a tablespoon or two of water to get the blender moving. (There may be no need to add water if you're using (thawed) frozen fruit or canned fruit).

4) Place the fruit in your blender. Now is the time to add the sweetener of your choice, if necessary.

5) After puréeing the fruit, you may choose to lightly wipe the fruit roll sheet with vegetable oil to help prevent sticking. Next: Simply pour the purée onto the food dehydrator's special fruit roll sheets – around 1.5 cups per tray.

6) Turn on your dehydrator and set the temperature between 135°F to 140°F. Note the higher temperature for fruit rolls!

7) Drying time: between 4 - 8 hours or until the fruit roll/leather is pliable (or per your food dehydrator's instructions). It should be non-sticky to the touch and a little shiny in appearance - and they do dry much browner, but that is absolutely nothing to worry about!

8) When the fruit roll has dried, peel it from the tray and roll it into a tight cylindrical shape. Use a piece of plastic wrap to wrap it up and store in airtight containers. At room temperature, they'll last a month. In my photo below, you'll see that I vacuum packed some so they will last even longer!

Remember to rotate your food dehydrator trays, for even drying.

Here are some fruit roll-ups, after vacuum-packing. These are ideal for backpacking – they're water-tight, air-tight – but remember to take some scissors along with you to open them!

12
DEHYDRATING GRAPES

Grapes – raisins in disguise! By dehydrating grapes to make raisins yourself, you'll find they taste better and plump up more than store-bought raisins. Raisins, as we all know, are a great handy snack – whether you are sat at home or are out backpacking in the great outdoors! Great nutrition for you and your kids...

Add grapes to fruit roll-ups too! Raisins are also great in breads and in your breakfast cereal... Grapes have been dried for thousands of years and have many hidden health benefits.

Grapes are a great source of vitamins A, C and K before they become raisins BUT when they ARE raisins, they have more Choline, Niacin, Folate, and Betaine, with higher trace amounts of Thiamin, and Riboflavin! In the mineral department, raisins beat grapes hands down in Potassium, Calcium, Magnesium, and Fluoride.

Both grapes and raisins contain Omega-3 and Omega-6 fatty acids

How to Dehydrate Grapes

Dehydrating grapes is very easy to do. Wash, remove the stems and cut in half or you may leave whole if desired. If you cut in half, place the grapes on the dehydrator sheet with the cut side facing up, so that the grape juice doesn't drip down to the trays below!
If you blanch the grapes first, see step one, below, you can save a ton of time in the dehydrator.

1) Rinse the grapes and blanch in a small amount of boiling water.

2) Cut the grapes in half and place on your food dehydrator sheets, cut-side up to prevent drips on the lower trays!

3) Turn on your dehydrator and set the temperature between 125°F and 135°F (or per your food dehydrator's instructions).

Drying time: between 6 – 10 hours

The raisins, er, dehydrated grapes will feel pliable when sufficiently dried.

Note: If drying your grapes whole, the drying time jumps to 10 – 36 hours so please bear that in mind. I highly recommend cutting the grapes in half! I did try the 'whole' method, but the trays got really sticky... and as stated, they took far longer to dehydrate... so cutting in half won out for me!

Remember to rotate your food dehydrator trays, for even drying.

For the green grapes, (see below), I decided to try just washing and slicing the grapes in half, without blanching first. They worked a treat! There's something about home-made raisins, they have that sweetness, but also a great tangy/tart taste too!

13
DEHYDRATING LEMONS
LIMES, AND ORANGES

Dehydrating Lemons, Limes, and Oranges are probably one of the easiest fruits to dehydrate, but probably not one of the most edible when dried, in my humble opinion! But having said that, let's not forget that dehydrated lemons, limes, and oranges can be great ground up to be used for flavorings and for baking!

If you remove the dehydrated rind and white pith, the dehydrated fruit centers make a tasty snack. The pith is the bitter tasting part of citrus.

Lemons have a high vitamin C content along with vitamin A, and in the mineral department they are high in Potassium and Calcium and also contain decent amounts of Magnesium and Phosphorus.

Limes are used very often in drinks and in the famous Key Lime Pie dessert!

Limes contain good amounts of Vitamins A and C and contain Folate and Choline too. In the mineral department Potassium, Calcium and Phosphorus are the leaders.

Oranges are loaded with vitamin C, plentiful vitamin A, and Folate. In the mineral department oranges score well in Calcium, Magnesium, Phosphorus, and Potassium. All three citrus fruits contain Omega-3 and Omega-6 fatty acids.

How to Dehydrate Citrus

1) Wash the skins of your citrus fruits.

2) Slice the citrus into 3/8" thick slices and arrange on your food dehydrator trays.

3) Turn on your food dehydrator and set the temperature between 125°F and 135°F (or per your food dehydrator's instructions). Drying time: between 2-12 hours.

Citrus is brittle when dried fully.

Please remember to rotate your dehydrator trays for even drying.

It's really amazing how light these orange slices feel after dehydrating!

14
DEHYDRATING MELONS

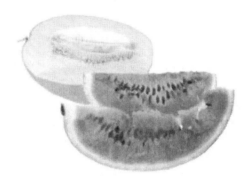

I have chosen two melons: the Honeydew and the good old drool-down-your-chin Watermelon! I mean, who can resist a huge slice of chilled watermelon, sitting by the pool with your feet dangling in the water? But watch out for those sticky drips...

There's a high vitamin A content and Folate, followed by vitamin C, and vitamin K in Honeydews. In the mineral department, honeydews are loaded with Potassium, followed by Phosphorous and Magnesium.

Honeydew melon is a good source of Omega-3 and Omega-6 fatty acids.

Watermelons are just as good too!

Watermelons also have a great vitamin A level, followed by vitamin C, Folate, and Choline. There are plenty of minerals to be found in watermelons: Phosphorous, Magnesium, Calcium, Potassium, and Fluoride!

Watermelon is a good source of carbohydrates too, and Omega-6 fatty acids.

How to Dehydrate Melons

1) Remove the skin and seeds from your honeydew or watermelon.

2) Slice the fruit into 1/2" thick slices and arrange on your food dehydrator trays.

3) Turn on your food dehydrator and set the temperature between 125°F and 135°F (or per your food dehydrator's instructions).

Drying time: between 8-20 hours.
Please remember to rotate your dehydrator trays for even drying.

NOTE: Don't toss the seeds. If you are inclined, you can roast the seeds.

- Let them dry thoroughly after giving them a cleaning in your sieve under the kitchen faucet.

- Spray the seeds first with plain cooking spray and a dash of salt.

• Toss them on a cookie sheet for 15 to 20 minutes at 325°F.

The seeds are best eaten when fully cooled.

Feel free to dehydrate Cantaloupes too!

They make great chips for snacking on when the kids get home from school!

15
DEHYDRATING PEACHES

Start dehydrating peaches for great snacks, cobblers, cookies, breads, and granola!

Peaches are high in vitamin A, and vitamin C, followed by vitamin K, Choline, and Folate.

In the mineral department, peaches are high in Potassium, followed by Phosphorus, Magnesium, Fluoride and Calcium. Peaches also contain Omega-3 and Omega-6 fatty acids too!

A few years ago, my husband and my mom went with me to visit Paula Deen's restaurant up in Savannah, Georgia. As we toured Georgia, we did NOT see one "Georgia Peaches for Sale" sign.

It was only on our way home when we came back into the
Florida panhandle did we actually see a
"Georgia Peaches for Sale" sign... do you think the
folk in Georgia know they're so good
and they were hiding them from us? :-)

How to Dehydrate Peaches

If using frozen peaches, ignore steps 1 and 2

1) Wash fresh peaches, peel if desired, remove the pit, and either slice in half, or cut into 1/4" slices.

2) Fresh peaches need to be pre-treated, so toss the peaches in a bowl and spray liberally with lemon juice TIP: Use a pump-top from a new unused spray bottle, pick one that fits your lemon juice bottle. Look for one that has a long enough plastic tube that'll reach to the bottom of your lemon juice bottle.

3) If you decided to simply cut your peaches in half, place them on your food dehydrator trays with the cut-side up to prevent drips on the lower trays!

4) Turn on your dehydrator and set the temperature between 125°F and 135°F (or per your food dehydrator's instructions).

Drying time: between 6-16 hours and they will feel pliable when dried.

Remember to rotate your food dehydrator trays, for even drying.

16
DEHYDRATING PEARS

Dehydrate pears when they are in season to enjoy all year long!

Pears contain vitamin A, and vitamin K, followed by vitamin C, Folate, and Choline.

In the mineral category, pears rank high in Potassium, followed by Phosphorus, Calcium, Magnesium, and Fluoride. Pears also contain Omega-6 fatty acids, and are a great source of carbohydrates and have a good amount of dietary fiber too!

Dehydrated pears are also tasty as snacks, cookies, fritters, breads, and granola. Also great in fruit rolls!

How to Dehydrate Pears

If using frozen pears, ignore steps 1 and 2

1) Wash fresh pears, peel if desired, remove the core, and either slice into halves, or quarters, or cut into 3/8" slices.

2) Fresh pears need to be pre-treated, so place the pears in a bowl and spray liberally with lemon juice -- TIP: Use a pump-top from a new unused spray bottle, pick one that fits your lemon juice bottle, look for one that has a long enough plastic tube that'll reach to the bottom of your lemon juice bottle. If you decided to simply cut your pears into halves or quarters, place them on your food dehydrator trays with the cut-side up to prevent drips on the lower trays!

3) Turn on your dehydrator and set the temperature between 125°F and 135°F (or per your food dehydrator's instructions).

Drying time for dehydrated pears: between 6-16 hours and they will feel pliable when dried.

Remember to rotate your food dehydrator trays, for even drying.

17
DEHYDRATING PLUMS

For great prunes, (yes they come from plums!), start by dehydrating plums! It's funny how a lot of people don't know what prunes really are -- but the cat is out of the bag now! :-)

Plums are high in vitamin A, followed by and vitamin C, vitamin K, Folate, and Choline.

In the mineral department, plums are high in Potassium, followed by Phosphorus, Magnesium, Calcium, Fluoride, and a trace amount of Iron. Plums also contain Omega-6 fatty acids too.

Plums are a great source of carbohydrates, and a decent amount of dietary fiber too and when dried as prunes, they are famous for their aid in our digestive-systems!

Just eat two or three a day and you'll be f-i-n-e !

According to Peggy Trowbridge Filippone, from About.com Home Cooking, prunes have a bad rep with younger folk, so the prune industry got together and re-named the prunes to 'dried plums'! (Original, huh?)

Dehydrated plums (prunes) are great for snacks, muffins, cookies, breads, and granola.

How to Dehydrate Plums

1) Wash fresh plums, remove the pit, and pop the back (see note below) to expose more of its surface to the air. Slice into halves or quarters.

2) Place your plums on your food dehydrator trays with the cut-side up to prevent drips on the lower trays!

3) Turn on your dehydrator and set the temperature between 125°F and 135°F (or per your food dehydrator's instructions).

Drying time: between 12-30 hours and they will be leathery in consistency when dried.

Remember to rotate your food dehydrator trays, for even drying.

NOTE: To "pop the back" means to turn the cut-in-half fruit 'inside out'. Use your thumb to push the skin inwards so that the flesh of the fruit is now on the outside.

18
DEHYDRATING RHUBARB

Rhubarb is a good source of vitamin A, and vitamin C, followed by Folate and Choline.

As far as minerals go, rhubarb is a fantastic source of Potassium and Calcium, followed by Phosphorus with trace amounts of Selenium, Iron, Manganese, and Zinc! Rhubarb also contains Omega-6 fatty acids.

Dehydrated rhubarb is great for pies, desserts, and tarts.

As a kid, I remember going to the back garden and climbing over the neighbor's fence -- to break off stalks of rhubarb from their abundant patch -- (the shame of it), and then rush home with the goodies...

Maybe this is something I should consider growing myself... then I don't have to scale walls and fences and get skinned knees! Back in the kitchen with ill-gotten rhubarb, I dipped the ends into sugar, and ate it raw. OMG. I used to eat too much of it and ended up with a stomach ache!

My dad told me he and his friends used to call it "yunky" - in a good way - when he was a kid - though he can't for the life of him remember *why* they called it that! :-)

How to Dehydrate Rhubarb

1) Rinse in water and then slice your rhubarb into 1" chunks.

2) Steam your rhubarb until it is slightly tender.

3) Place the rhubarb on your food dehydrator trays.

4) Turn on your dehydrator and set the temperature between 125°F and 135°F (or per your food dehydrator's instructions).

Drying time: between 6-14 hours.

Dehydrated rhubarb will feel leathery when dried.

Remember to rotate your food dehydrator trays, for even drying.

19
DEHYDRATING STRAWBERRIES

Dehydrating strawberries is easy and are great for snacks, baked goods, and cereal topping.

Strawberries are high in vitamin A, vitamin C, followed by Choline and vitamin K. There are trace amounts of vitamin E, Betaine, Pantothenic Acid, Niacin and vitamin B6.

In the mineral department, strawberries are high in Potassium, followed by Phosphorus, Calcium, Magnesium, and Fluoride. Strawberries have trace amounts of Selenium, Manganese, Iron, and Copper. Strawberries contain Omega-3 and Omega-6 fatty acids too.

Obtaining strawberries fresh from "You Pick 'Em" farms, is probably the best way to go of obtaining sweet big strawberries... so long as you don't 'put your back out' bending down! It's a great activity for the kids (read: have 'them' do the bending down!)

Strawberries are easy to grow in pots, or in beds, no matter the size of your backyard.

How to Dehydrate Strawberries

If using frozen strawberries, slice them when they are partially thawed -- then go to step 2.

1) Wash fresh strawberries, cut off the top, and cut into 1/4" slices or into halves.

2) If you decided to simply cut your strawberries in half, place them on your food dehydrator trays with the cut-side up to prevent drips on the lower trays!

3) Turn on your dehydrator and set the temperature between 125°F and 135°F (or per your food dehydrator's instructions).

Drying time: between 6-15 hours.

Dehydrated strawberries will be crisp and leathery when dried.

Remember to rotate your food dehydrator trays, for even drying.

Check out what dehydrated strawberries look like, on the next page.

Dehydrated Strawberries on an Excalibur
Dehydrator Tray

20
YOUR DEHYDRATING VEGGIES HQ

Eat Your Veggies!
How often did you hear that growing up?

Dehydrating veggies, whether they are fresh from the grocery store or your garden, gives you your own private stock of peas, corn, celery, potatoes, etc. on hand -- all year 'round!

When you bring your fresh veggies indoors, you can attend to them right away... get them washed, and dehydrated.

Trust me, this saves you valuable prep time in the kitchen at mealtimes.

You can easily throw together a very satisfying vegetable soup in less than ten minutes tops!

Pick a Vegetable

(GREEN) BEANS

BROCCOLI

BUTTERNUT SQUASH

CABBAGE

CARROTS

CAULIFLOWER

CELERY

CORN

GARLIC

MUSHROOMS

ONIONS

PEAS

PEPPERS

POTATOES

TOMATOES

ZUCCHINI

How Many Fresh Vegetables Should I Buy to Fill 4 Dehydrator Trays?

An Easy Guide for Vegetables

Most of us do not have tons of spare room in our fridges and freezers, so before you go out buying too much, here's a handy guide that shows you roughly how many vegetables will fit on four dehydrator trays. Please remember this is just a guide. It's not an exact science...

VEGETABLES

Cut Green Beans: fresh or frozen, 2lb
Broccoli: fresh or frozen, 2lbs
Butternut Squash: fresh, 1 medium squash; frozen 2lb
Cabbage: fresh sliced, 1/2 cabbage head
Carrots: fresh, sliced 5-8 carrots; frozen 2lb
Cauliflower: fresh, 1 medium; frozen 2lb
Celery: fresh, 1 stalk, sliced
Cut Corn: fresh: 6-8 ears; frozen 2lb
Garlic: Elephant, fresh: 1 large bulb
Mushrooms: fresh, 2lb
Onions: fresh 1-1/2 to 2 medium to large; diced frozen 2lb
Peas: fresh or frozen 2lb

Peppers: fresh, cut in strips 4-5; frozen 2lb
Potatoes: fresh, varies 4-6; frozen diced hash brown 2lb
Tomatoes: fresh, 7-9
Zucchini: fresh, 3-6

What's The Ideal Temperature To Use for Dehydrating Vegetables?

Vegetables are best dehydrated between 125°F and 135°F – any hotter than that and you may cause the dehydrated vegetables to get a hard crust - this is known as 'case hardening' and we need to prevent this from occurring. Case hardening prevents the inside of the vegetable from drying properly so don't be tempted to turn the food dehydrator on high to speed up the process!

Preparation for Dehydrating Vegetables

Some vegetables can be washed and sliced and dried with no further preparation necessary. All frozen vegetables can be placed on your dehydrator trays with no further preparation.

Select a vegetable you wish to dehydrate from the list, a few pages back. Each vegetable has full dehydrating instructions, specific to your vegetable selection.

Before opening your bag of frozen vegetables, throw the bag onto your kitchen counter-top a few times to loosen any frozen vegetables that may have frozen together in a clump! If you have a few small persistent clumps, run the clump under cold water for a few seconds and that will fix it!

Or even easier than all that -- leave the bag of frozen vegetables unopened in your kitchen sink for about an hour and they'll be good for slicing.

Certain vegetables, like fresh carrots, need to have a generous spraying of lemon juice. We use lemon juice as a totally acceptable substitute for ascorbic acid (which is used by professional dehydrating plants), and lemon juice works wonderfully!

Two reasons for spraying with lemon juice:

1) prevent the vegetables from darkening

2) prevent bacterial growth during drying

Dehydrated Veggies are Dry When...

...they don't stick together! If you think your dehydrated vegetables are dried enough, place the dehydrated vegetables in airtight bags (such as zip-lock bags), and let them hang around your kitchen for a day or overnight.

This is known as conditioning (see page 134) and this enables the air and any moisture in the bag to distribute evenly – so that the dehydrated vegetables will be ready for vacuum sealing!

21
DEHYDRATING (GREEN) BEANS

Dehydrating beans, whether fresh or frozen, is easy to do and green beans are certainly most people's favorite veggie... you know, at Christmas time, the green bean casserole! Green beans are great in homemade soups... I love them year 'round!

Nothing tastes better than home-grown green beans, but for ease right now of getting some put away quickly, I used frozen green beans, straight from the bag - no preparation necessary! How easy is that?

If your frozen beans are clumping, let them sit in the kitchen sink, unopened, for about an hour. Or you can simply drop the unopened bag on the kitchen counter-top a few times to loosen them. This works for me!

Green beans are high in vitamin A, Choline and vitamin C, followed by Folate and vitamin K. Green Beans rank high in these minerals: Potassium, Calcium, Phosphorus, Fluoride, and Magnesium. Trace minerals are Iron, Selenium, and Zinc, Manganese, and Copper. There are also Omega-3 and Omega-6 fatty acids in green beans.

How to Dehydrate Green Beans

If using frozen green beans, ignore steps 1 and 2.

1) Gently wash fresh green beans. Trim off the ends.

2) Blanch in a small amount of boiling water for about 3 minutes.

3) Arrange the green beans on your dehydrator trays, making sure the beans don't overlap.

4) Turn on your food dehydrator and set the temperature between 125°F and 135°F (or per your food dehydrator's instructions).

Drying time: between 6-8 hours.

Green beans will feel tough and brittle when dried.

Please remember to rotate your dehydrator trays for even drying.

Here's what dehydrated green beans look like,
they are quite brittle when fully dried.

22
DEHYDRATING BROCCOLI

Dehydrating broccoli is easy whether you're using fresh or frozen! The only problem with frozen broccoli that I've noticed is that it tends to be very bitty - i.e. there's not usually plenty of broccoli florets, or spears as they are also known, (maybe I need to spend more on a better quality brand?)... *anyway*...

Frozen broccoli is a great stand-in for fresh when it's out of season, as we all love fresh broccoli when it's tossed raw in salads or used as a dipper during summer! Avoid the solid blocks of broccoli, buy the bags of loose florets. How about broccoli with cheese! Yummy!

Did you know that broccoli has been around for over 2000 years and counting!

Broccoli is a good source of vitamin A, vitamin K, vitamin C, folate, Choline and has trace amounts of Niacin, Vitamin E, Thiamin. Broccoli's minerals are Potassium, Phosphorus, Calcium, and Magnesium. Trace minerals are Iron, Zinc, Manganese, and Selenium. Broccoli also contains Omega-3 and Omega-6 fatty acids too.

How to Dehydrate Broccoli

NOTE: if your frozen broccoli has clumped together in the bag, prior to opening the bag drop it gently on your counter-top a few times -- this helps to loosen it up!

If you still have a few small clumps on your dehydrator trays, simply run the clumps under clean cool water for a few seconds, and that'll do the trick! Or leave broccoli unopened in the bag in the kitchen sink for an hour, you will be able to slice the big florets very easily after that.

If using frozen broccoli, ignore steps 1 and 2.

1) Thoroughly wash your fresh broccoli. Cut into small florets. The broccoli looks like miniature bushes now!

2) Blanch in a small amount of boiling water for about 2 minutes. Look how nice and bright the color is! OK, if they're too big, slice in half so they fit easily on your trays.

3) Arrange the broccoli spears on your dehydrator trays, making sure they don't touch each other - give them some breathing room.

4) Turn on your food dehydrator and set the temperature between 125°F and 135°F (or per your food dehydrator's instructions) and that's all there is to it!

When your dehydrated broccoli is fully dried, it will be appear very brittle.

Drying time for broccoli: between 6-14 hours.

Please remember to rotate your dehydrator trays for evenly dehydrated broccoli florets.

Dehydrated Broccoli is very versatile...

When dried broccoli is re-hydrated, it is superb as broccoli soup, as well as a soufflé and works well as a sauce! And let's not forget to add broccoli in quiches too! Granted, it isn't as good as fresh, but it's a close second... and that's why dehydrated broccoli works well in soups and sauces.

Add dried broccoli to your arsenal of dehydrated vegetables - so you won't run out! It's a nutritional powerhouse. If your kids see you eating broccoli and actually enjoying it, you stand a better chance of your kids eating it too! :-)

You can even start growing your own broccoli, and eat the sprouts! broccoli sprouts are loaded with nutrients the body needs...

23
DEHYDRATING BUTTERNUT SQUASH

Dehydrating butternut squash takes a little prep work but is loaded with vitamin A, followed by vitamin C, Folate, vitamin E, vitamin K, Niacin, and trace amounts of Pantothenic Acid and Thiamin, so it's well worth your time and energy.

In the butternut squash's mineral department, potassium ranks high, followed by calcium, magnesium, phosphorus, with trace amounts of selenium, manganese, and zinc. Butternut squash also contains Omega-3 and Omega-6 fatty acids too.

Although butternut squash can be difficult to peel, it's well worth the effort!

This vegetable needs to be steamed lightly first, to aid in the dehydrating process

Butternut squash makes a great soup, and purées well for sauces, and I use it for my Chicken Chow dog food... make YOUR dog very happy too by using our free recipe!

How to Dehydrate Butternut Squash

If using frozen butternut squash, ignore steps 1 and 2.

I'd like to make a note here that I have not tried dehydrating puréed frozen butternut squash, but I think it would work just fine on the fruit roll sheets! All you need to do is let it thaw out first so you can spread it.

1) Peel the butternut squash and cut into 3/4 inch strips, or cubed butternut squash is fine for more even drying.

2) Steam over boiling water for about 7 minutes, or until your squash is tender.

3) Arrange the butternut squash on your dehydrator trays, making sure they don't overlap each other.

4) Turn on your food dehydrator and set the temperature between 125°F and 135°F (or per your food dehydrator's instructions) and that's all there is to it!

Drying time: between 7-10 hours.

Butternut squash will be leathery in consistency when dried.

Please remember to rotate your dehydrator trays for even drying.

You can also dehydrate Acorn Squash the same way.

24
DEHYDRATING CABBAGE

Dehydrating Cabbage: Yes, it can be done and is a vegetable that doesn't immediately spring to mind as being able to dehydrate -- because it seems so dry to begin with... yet it can be done quite easily!

A plus when slicing is that one head of cabbage goes a very long way... and it's a great source of vitamin A, vitamin K, and Folate. It's not lacking in the mineral department either: it's a great source of Potassium and a good source of Calcium, Phosphorus with trace minerals Selenium, Zinc, and Manganese. Cabbage also contains Omega-6 fatty acids too.

I love to add shredded dehydrated cabbage to my vegetable soups, just drop it in - it's that easy - and it cooks along with the rest of the vegetables.

How to Dehydrate Cabbage

1) There's not much preparation; simply remove the outer leaves (these can be saved for making stuffed cabbage rolls for instance) and rinse if necessary under cold water. Start slicing it into thin strips, about 1/8" wide.

2) Arrange on your food dehydrator trays. The cabbage may overlap a bit, but that's OK.

3) Turn on your food dehydrator and set the temperature between 125°F and 135°F (or per your food dehydrator's instructions).

Fully dehydrated cabbage will be brittle when fully dried.

Drying time: between 7-11 hours.

Please remember to rotate your dehydrator trays, for even drying.

7 trays of Cabbage!

25
DEHYDRATING CARROTS

Dehydrating carrots is easy to do and carrots are well-known for their great source of beta carotene (Vitamin A), and are a great source of Folate, and Vitamin K.

Carrots rank well for their mineral content: Calcium, Phosphorus, Potassium, and Magnesium. Carrots' trace minerals are Fluoride, Zinc, Manganese, Selenium, and Copper...

...and they give you orange hands when handling,
so use those latex gloves for protection...
and to keep your germs off the carrots!

Carrots contain Omega-3 and Omega-6 fatty acids too.

Check out our fantastic carrot soup recipe, either make it from fresh or dehydrated carrots, plus we have Debby's Delectable Carrot Cake to share with you too – both of which are in the Recipes section!

If you want to have dehydrated carrots put away for making the carrot cake at a later date, then I strongly suggest using the fruit roll sheets to keep the finely grated carrots from falling through the food dehydrator trays, but it will add a little to the drying time. I prefer to use fresh whole carrots and slice them after peeling, but you can use whole frozen baby carrots with great results. Frozen carrots are a great stand-in and require absolutely NO preparation! Fresh carrots need peeling then slicing, or grating, and I highly recommend a mandoline for the slicing but BE CAREFUL with them... they're very sharp!

When you have finished slicing or grating, place the carrots in a glass bowl (or any non-plastic bowl) and spray with lemon juice, tossing the carrots as you go to make sure they're sprayed evenly. TIP: Use a pump-top from a new unused spray bottle, pick one that fits your lemon juice bottle. Look for a bottle that has a long enough plastic tube that will reach to the bottom of your lemon juice bottle.

NOTE: If you choose to blanch your sliced carrots in a small amount of boiling water for about 3 minutes, there's no need to use lemon juice.

How to Dehydrate Carrots

1) Arrange your sliced carrots on your food dehydrator trays, leave space between the carrots so they're not touching each other, to allow the warm air to do its job. If dehydrating grated carrots, spread them out as much as possible on your fruit roll trays (or use plastic wrap AND cut out A HOLE in the center for the air to circulate if using a Nesco dehydrator).

2) Turn on your food dehydrator and set the temperature between 125°F and 135°F (or per your food dehydrator's instructions).

Dehydrated carrots will be leathery when fully dried.

Drying time: between 6 -12 hours.

Please remember to rotate your dehydrator trays, for even drying and place any larger carrot pieces on the outside edges of the dehydrator tray.

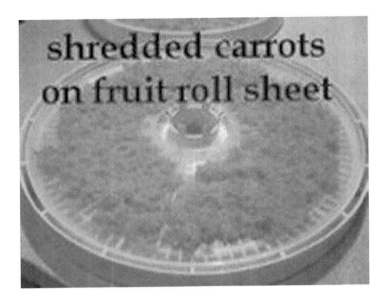

Shredded carrots are great for making Deb's Delectable Carrot Cake,
see recipe on page 256

26
DEHYDRATING CAULIFLOWER

Dehydrating cauliflower when it's in season
enables you to make delicious Cauliflower Soup
and Cauliflower Mash all year long!

Add millet and quinoa (see page 279) to the Cauliflower Mash -- kids
like this, as it compares favorably to 'mashed potatoes'... the millet
and quinoa really adds to the goodness of cauliflower!

Cauliflower is a good source of vitamins A and C, and Choline, followed by Pantothenic Acid, Vitamin B6, Niacin, Riboflavin, with trace amounts of vitamin E, and vitamin K.

In the mineral department, cauliflower is rich in Potassium, followed by Phosphorus, Calcium, and Magnesium.

There are trace amounts of Selenium, Iron, Zinc, Manganese, and Fluoride.

Cauliflower contains Omega-3 and Omega-6 fatty acids.

How to Dehydrate Cauliflower

NOTE: You will have to slice the larger cauliflower pieces in half so that the cauliflower will fit between the food dehydrator trays.

Let the cauliflower thaw out (in its bag, unopened) in your kitchen sink in a bowl of tepid water if you're short on time, otherwise let the cauliflower bag thaw out for around an hour in your kitchen sink, unopened, then chop and put on the trays.

If thawing the frozen cauliflower by the water-in-the-bowl method, keep changing out the tepid water in the bowl until the cauliflower has thawed sufficiently for you to be able to cut (feel the pieces while they're still in the bag until they're soft enough). This will probably take about 10 minutes.

If using frozen cauliflower, ignore steps 1 and 2.

1) Wash and slice fresh cauliflower into 1/2" thick pieces.

2) Blanch the cauliflower in a small amount of boiling water for a few minutes, in batches.

3) Arrange on your food dehydrator trays, making sure the cauliflower pieces don't touch, for good air circulation.

4) Turn on your food dehydrator and set the temperature between 125°F and 135°F (or per your food dehydrator's instructions).

Dehydrated cauliflower will be brittle when fully dried.

Drying time: between 6-14 hours.

Please remember to rotate your trays for even drying.

Don't worry if your cauliflower turns a little brown, this is a natural occurrence when dehydrating and is nothing to worry about.

27
DEHYDRATING CELERY

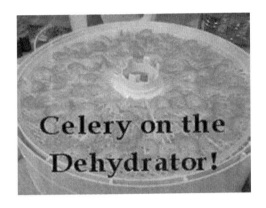

Make great tasting soups by dehydrating celery!

I have a couple of easy celery-based soups for you to wrap your taste-buds around: Celery and Potato Soup and a Curried version! Please save the celery leaves, they are great chopped up and added to soups; also, don't discard the tiny part of the celery stalks, these chop up great and can be added to Tuna and Chicken Salads! (All recipes are in the Recipe Section, starting on page 197).

Celery is a good source of vitamin A, followed by Choline, vitamin C, Niacin, Pantothenic Acid.

There are trace amounts of Riboflavin, vitamin B6, Betaine, Folate, and vitamin K. In the mineral department, celery is rich in Potassium, Calcium, Magnesium, and Phosphorus.

There are also trace amounts of Iron, Selenium, Zinc, Manganese, and Fluoride. Celery contains Omega-6 fatty acids.

Dehydrated celery is fantastic re-hydrated - it plumps up really well and you can't tell the difference from fresh! Great for stews and soups!

You can grind it up too to make your own celery salt (add equal parts of salt and celery!)

How to Dehydrate Celery

1) Wash and slice fresh celery into 1/8" thick slices, a mandoline does a fine job of this – just watch your fingers please!

2) Arrange on your food dehydrator trays, making sure the celery slices don't touch.

3) Turn on your food dehydrator and set the temperature between 125°F and 135°F (or per your food dehydrator's instructions).

Dehydrated celery will be leathery when fully dried.

Drying time: between 3-10 hours.

Please remember to rotate your trays for even drying.

Dehydrated celery reminds me of tiny seahorses
for some strange reason...
yes, people do wonder about me :-)

28
DEHYDRATING CORN

Corn is a great source of fiber – fabulous in Vegetable Soup or as a Chowder! Let's get busy dehydrating some – by using bags of Frozen corn! How easy is that?

Dehydrated corn is great for use in vegetable soups and stews, fritters, or as a corn chowder!

You can grind it into cornmeal! Frozen corn has got to be right up there with frozen peas for ease of dehydrating!

There's no excuse for not dehydrating corn...

Frozen off-the-cob corn is a great source of vitamin A, followed by Choline, vitamin C, and Niacin. There are trace amounts of vitamin E, Thiamin, Riboflavin, Pantothenic Acid, and Folate. In the mineral department, frozen corn is a good source of Potassium, Phosphorus, Magnesium, followed by Calcium, and Iron. There are trace amounts of Zinc Manganese, Copper, and Fluoride.

Frozen corn contains Omega-3 fatty acids and a high amount of Omega-6 fatty acids too!

Corn is rich in starch and dietary fiber - and the fiber is good news for a stubborn digestive system...

How to Dehydrate Corn

Here are instructions for FROZEN corn, remember, we're all about "the easy" here! (See next page for Fresh Corn).

1) Toss your frozen bag of corn kernels on the counter top a few times to loosen the kernels

2) Arrange the frozen corn on your food dehydrator trays, making sure there's some space for breathing room!

3) Turn on your food dehydrator and set the temperature between 125°F and 135°F (or per your food dehydrator's instructions).

Dehydrated corn will be brittle when fully dried.

Drying time: between 6-12 hours.

Please remember to rotate your trays for even drying.

Fresh Corn

For those of you with fresh corn, simply husk and wash them.

1) Get a pan of water boiling and steam the ears for 4-5 minutes. Get them into cold water as soon as possible to stop the cooking process.

2) Next, cut the corn off the cob by standing the ear on its end, and slice downwards from the top to cut off the kernels.

3) Arrange the corn on the dehydrator trays.

4) Turn on your food dehydrator and set the temperature between 125°F and 135°F (or per your food dehydrator's instructions).

Make sure you get the whole kernel and not tons of stalk!

Fresh corn takes around 12-15 hours when fully dehydrated.

It will be brittle and very hard.

29
DEHYDRATING GARLIC

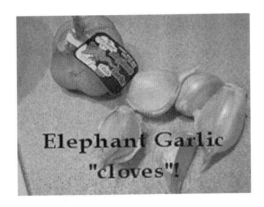

Dehydrating garlic is easy when you use Elephant Garlic!

Garlic is a great source of vitamin A, vitamin C, and vitamin B6, followed by Choline. There are trace amounts of vitamin K, Folate, Niacin, Thiamin, Riboflavin, and Pantothenic Acid.

Elephant (often called mammoth) garlic is a good source of Potassium, Phosphorus, and Calcium, followed by Iron and Manganese. There are trace amounts of Zinc, Copper, and Selenium.

Garlic contains Omega-3 and Omega-6 fatty acids.

Elephant Garlic is a
milder version of regular garlic

Garlic is great for use in tons of recipes: Soups and stews, Italian dishes of all types! If you're out on a date, then make sure both partners eat garlic, you'll thank each other later for that tip! Dehydrated garlic can also be ground up for use as garlic powder! Add equal amounts of salt and ground garlic powder and you now have Garlic Salt.

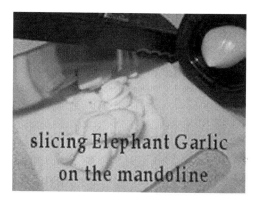

NOTE: When dehydrating garlic, you may want to consider dehydrating some onions at the same time if you've got a spare dehydrator tray or two available!

Don't mix garlic and onions with, say, apples, when dehydrating – unless you WANT your APPLES to taste like GARLIC or ONIONS!

How to Dehydrate Garlic

1) Separate and peel the cloves, cut into 1/8" slices - a mandoline does a fine job of this for the elephant garlic - just watch your fingers please! With regular (small) garlic cloves, carefully use a knife!

2) Arrange on your food dehydrator trays, making sure the garlic slices don't touch.

3) Turn on your food dehydrator and set the temperature between 125°F and 135°F (or per your food dehydrator's instructions).

Garlic will be brittle when fully dried. I store my dehydrated garlic in a small mason jar, and crumble it up when adding to my soups etc.

Drying time for garlic: between 6-12 hours.

Please remember to rotate your trays for even drying.

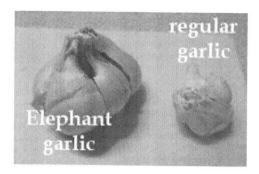

If you've ever seen the movie "Crocodile Dundee"
when he was being robbed in New York
and the robber brandished what the robber considered
to be a big knife... and then Crocodile Dundee
pulled out his 'big knife'...

then you'll appreciate this comment about
regular garlic versus Mammoth Garlic:
(pointing to the regular garlic)

"You call that garlic?"

(now pointing to the elephant garlic)

"Now That's Garlic!" :-)

30
DEHYDRATING MUSHROOMS

ready-sliced mushrooms
on the dehydrator tray

Dehydrating mushrooms takes special care; don't wash them
as that will make them too wet... and mushrooms are
dehydrated on <u>two</u> different temperature settings,
see "How-To" instructions, next page.

Mushrooms are used in many recipes: Cream of Mushroom Soup,
and added to Stews, Omelets, and as Pizza toppings! Back in the UK,
I loved mushrooms on toast! *(I'll have to hunt out that recipe, now that I've
had my short trip down memory lane here!)*

White mushrooms contain vitamin D, vitamin C, Choline, Folate, Betaine, and Niacin, followed by trace amounts of Pantothenic Acid, Riboflavin, Thiamin, and vitamin B6.

In the mineral department, white mushrooms are a good source of Potassium, Phosphorus, followed by Magnesium and Calcium. There are trace amounts of Iron, Zinc, Copper, and Selenium in mushrooms too.

White mushrooms contain Omega-6 fatty acids.

How to Dehydrate Mushrooms

1) Use pre-sliced mushrooms for convenience. If you're using whole mushrooms, gently wipe the mushrooms with a clean damp cloth first to clean them. That's all you need to do.

2) If whole, slice from the cap top down through the stem, into 3/8" slices.

3) Arrange your sliced mushrooms on your food dehydrator trays, making sure the mushroom slices don't overlap.

4) SPECIAL NOTE for MUSHROOMS: Turn on your food dehydrator at 90°F for Excalibur dehydrators, and 95°F for Nesco dehydrators - for two to three hours THEN set the temperature to 125°F and dry for the remaining time.

Dehydrated mushrooms will be leathery when fully dried.

Drying time: 3 hours at low temperature, then up to 10 hours on the higher temperature.

Please remember to rotate your trays for even drying.

NOTE: Don't be fooled by the first drying. After conditioning, they may still be quite 'damp' -- so don't be afraid to really dry them out and giving them another go-around for an hour or two in the dehydrator!

31
DEHYDRATING ONIONS

Dehydrating onions can be a tearful job, and please run your range hood vent (if you have one) and place your dehydrator close to it... that will help enormously to take the onion odor out of the kitchen!

Onion is a great source of vitamin A, followed by vitamin C. There are trace amounts of Niacin, Pantothenic Acid, vitamin B6, Riboflavin, and Thiamin.

Onion's minerals: a great source of Potassium, followed by Phosphorus, and Calcium.

There are trace amounts of Iron, Zinc, Manganese, Copper, and Selenium too. Onion contains Omega-3 and Omega-6 fatty acids.

Frozen chopped onions are so e-a-s-y to use! Onions are great for use in many recipes: soups and stews, you name it! You can grind them up for use as onion powder too!

NOTE: When dehydrating onion, you may want to consider dehydrating some garlic at the same time if you've got a spare dehydrator tray or two available.

Don't mix onions and garlic with, say, apples, when dehydrating -- unless you WANT your APPLES to taste like ONIONS or GARLIC!!

As mentioned previously, you may also wish to have your windows OPEN, or put the A/C on while you're dehydrating... as the onion-odor can certainly circulate throughout the whole house! If you ABSOLUTELY LOVE onions it's not such a bad thing... but if you don't...!

Also, be aware that onion odor is not good for pets. Please don't let this put you off dehydrating onions, though; I just want you to know about the odor and pets in advance.

How to Dehydrate Onions

If using frozen onions, ignore step 1.

1) Peel and slice into 3/8" slices (or rings or diced!)

2) Arrange on your food dehydrator trays, try to make sure they don't overlap.

3) Turn on your food dehydrator and set the temperature between 125°F and 135°F (or per your food dehydrator's instructions).

Dehydrated onion will be leathery when fully dried.

Drying time: between 4-12 hours.

Please remember to rotate your trays for even drying.

32
DEHYDRATING PEAS

Dehydrating peas is one of the easiest
of all vegetables to dehydrate -
they rank right up there with corn!

Simply use frozen peas, straight from the grocery store -- or if you're lucky and have your own garden, dehydrate your fresh peas! Peas are great for use in soups and stews! I love to eat them with mashed potatoes – my dad (when I was a kid) used to put mash on his fork, turn it upside down and dip it into the peas! *It's a great way to get peas to stay on your fork!)*

I have two great pea soup recipes for you! Velvety Pea Soup is one of my dad's favorite soups that I make and the other is Green Split Pea Soup made in the slow cooker. (See recipes section, starting on page 197).

Peas are a fantastic source of vitamin A, followed by vitamin C, Choline, and Niacin. There are trace amounts of Thiamin, Pantothenic Acid, Riboflavin, vitamin B6, and vitamin K. Minerals found in peas: a good source of Potassium, followed by Phosphorus, Magnesium, and Calcium.

Peas have trace amounts of Iron, Zinc, Manganese, Copper, and Selenium. Peas also contain Omega-3 and Omega-6 fatty acids.

How to Dehydrate Peas

Yes I use frozen peas all the time -- so E-A-S-Y!!!

If you are using frozen peas, ignore step 1.

For those of you lucky enough to grow your own:

1) Shell, wash, and lightly steam fresh peas until you see the skin indent a little, then rinse with cold water, let dry.

2) Arrange on your food dehydrator trays, making sure the peas have some breathing room!

3) Turn on your food dehydrator and set the temperature between 125°F and 135°F (or per your food dehydrator's instructions).

Dehydrated peas will be brittle when fully dried.

Drying time: between 5-14 hours.

Please remember to rotate your trays for even drying.

Peas dehydrating on the Nesco

33
DEHYDRATING PEPPERS

Dehydrating Peppers takes a few easy steps and are great for use in stir-fry dishes, and omelets to name a few uses! Frozen peppers can be used too!

Peppers are not only colorful, they are a fantastic source of vitamin A with red peppers being #1. The vitamin C leader is the yellow pepper!

The champion Folate pepper is the red pepper! All three contain trace amounts of Niacin, vitamin B6, and Pantothenic Acid. Minerals found in all three peppers: a good source of Potassium, followed by Phosphorus, Magnesium, and Calcium. There are trace amounts of Iron, Zinc, Manganese, and Copper. Selenium can be found in the red and yellow peppers, and Fluoride only in the green pepper!

Green and red, but not yellow Peppers, contain Omega-3 and Omega-6 fatty acids.

Peppers Ready for Dehydrating

How to Dehydrate Peppers

If using frozen peppers, ignore step 1.

1) Remove the stem and seeds from the peppers and slice into 1/4" strips.

2) Arrange the sliced peppers on your food dehydrator trays, making sure the peppers don't overlap.

3) Turn on your food dehydrator and set the temperature between 125°F and 135°F (or per your food dehydrator's instructions).

Fully dehydrated peppers will be leathery when dried.

Drying time: between 4-12 hours.

Please remember to rotate your trays for even drying.

In my photos below, you'll see that I have made three separate bags with a combination of yellow, green, and red peppers - perfect for a stir-fry or omelet! Simply re-hydrate!

Three Peppers Dehydrated In A Vacuum Pack!

These fresh peppers were originally store-bought three-to-a-pack, and the left-side of the photo above shows nine peppers total, so you can see how much room you can save by dehydrating the peppers!

In the same photo but on the right-hand side, you can see a packet. This is a 100cc oxygen pack. The package shows one vacuum-packed bag of peppers.

34
DEHYDRATING POTATOES

slicing cooked and chilled potatoes

Dehydrating potatoes can be done either by using fresh potatoes, or you can cheat by using frozen (diced) hash browns, or grated hash browns – now that's easy!

TIP: if using frozen hash browns, drop the frozen unopened bag on the kitchen counter-top a few times to break up any clumps. If clumps persist, run the clump under cool running water for a few seconds -- that should do the trick!

Potatoes are everyone's favorites and I'll show you
how they can be easily dehydrated from pre-cooked,
sliced potatoes! The hash brown variety is great
in vegetable soups, and the sliced potatoes make a
mean Potato and Bacon Hash – see our recipes section!

Potatoes are loaded with a range of vitamins: vitamin A, vitamin C, and Choline, followed by Niacin, Thiamin, vitamin B6, Pantothenic Acid, and Betaine.

Trace amounts of vitamin K, and Folate. Minerals to be found in potatoes are Potassium, followed by Phosphorus, Magnesium, and Calcium. There are trace amounts of Iron, Zinc, Manganese, Copper and Selenium. Potatoes contain Omega-3 and Omega-6 fatty acids too.

How to Dehydrate Potatoes

If using frozen hash brown potatoes, simply ignore steps 1, 2, and 3.

1) Gently scrub and wash potatoes in the sink.

2) Put in a pan of water, NO SALT, and bring to a boil, simmer for 20 minutes.

3) Place potatoes in a bowl, and when cooled off, put in the refrigerator overnight. This helps tremendously when you slice them tomorrow into 3/8" slices! I leave the skins on, as there are loads of nutrients in the skins too.

4) Arrange the potatoes on your food dehydrator trays, making sure the potatoes don't overlap.

5) Turn on your food dehydrator and set the temperature between 125°F and 135°F (or per your food dehydrator's instructions).

Potatoes will be leathery and/or brittle when fully dried.

Drying time for potatoes: between 6-14 hours.

Please remember to rotate your trays for even drying.

Here is another way to store potatoes: freeze them. Joan, fondly known as the "Case Hardened Lady" wrote in to the site (www.easy-food-dehydrating.com) to tell us how she prepares her potatoes for dehydrating. Here it is, straight from Joan:

"Started batch number four of potatoes this morning. Things are running quickly and smoothly now that I have the routine down. Still forget to start heating the blanching water first though -- it takes about 20 minutes on my stove.

"I'm doing sliced raw potatoes. Anyway in my mind it takes longer to peel and slice potatoes than to get the water boiling. In reality it's only a few minutes of prep, then potatoes are ready and the water isn't.

"Oh, what a journey these 99 cent bags of potatoes have taken me on!"

Thanks for writing in Joan! - Susan

Photo below shows sliced dehydrated potatoes after being vacuum-sealed, along with a 100cc oxypack: look closely under the "P" in Potatoes... that is an oxypack!

Read more about their function in the Oxygen Absorbers chapter in our storing dehydrated food for the long-term section on page 137.

35
DEHYDRATING TOMATOES

Imagine this: While dehydrating tomatoes, their vitamin C, vitamin K, Thiamin, and Niacin, along with Folate, and Cholate, content increases!

Tomatoes are a fantastic source of vitamin A, followed by vitamin C, and Choline. Trace vitamins are: Niacin, and vitamin E, along with Thiamin, and Betaine, Pantothenic Acid, Folate, and vitamin K.

Minerals to be found in tomatoes are: Potassium, Phosphorus, Magnesium, and Calcium. There are trace amounts of Iron, Zinc, Manganese, and Copper. Tomatoes contain Omega-3 and Omega-6 fatty acids.

Tomatoes are great for many recipes, and for sauces, and puréeing. Make them into a powder in your blender and add water to make a paste!

When made into a sauce, consider pouring the sauce onto the special roll up sheets and make a 'tomato roll up/leather'. This way, you can store it away for use later, maybe as a pizza or as spaghetti sauce!

How to Dehydrate Tomatoes

1) Wash and slice the tomatoes into 3/8" slices. You may first dip them into boiling water to make skin removal easier if you wish to skin them. For cherry tomatoes, cut in half, no skinning required.

2) Arrange the tomatoes on your food dehydrator trays, making sure the tomato slices don't overlap - or if using the cherry tomato halves, place them cut side up to prevent dripping to the lower trays.

3) Turn on your food dehydrator and set the temperature between 125°F and 135°F (or per your food dehydrator's instructions).

Tomatoes will be leathery or brittle when fully dried.

Drying time for tomatoes: between 5-12 hours.

Please remember to rotate your trays for even drying.

~*~

Many folk pack their dried tomatoes in olive oil, with added herbs. Store in glass jars – and there you have your own 'sundried' tomatoes in oil – very tasty! The tomatoes will plump back up, given time, in the oil.

36
DEHYDRATING ZUCCHINI

Dehydrating Zucchini is very easy and makes fantastic zucchini bread, can be added to soups, and casseroles or as a dip for chips. How about a cream sauce, or battered and fried zucchini?

I love zucchini in Ratatouille (see Recipe Section starting on page 200), which is a dish comprised of onions, squash, zucchini, black olives, Italian herbs, tomatoes... You can use either fresh or dehydrated zucchini and I'll show you how easy it is!

There's not much preparation necessary for zucchini aside from washing it in cool, clean water!

Zucchini is a good source of vitamin A, vitamin C, and Choline, followed by Niacin, Pantothenic Acid, vitamin B6, and Riboflavin. Trace vitamins are Folate, and vitamin K.

Minerals found in zucchini are: Potassium, Phosphorus, Magnesium, and Calcium, followed by Zinc, Iron, Manganese, and Copper.

There are trace amounts of Selenium. Zucchini contain Omega-3 and Omega-6 fatty acids.

How to Dehydrate Zucchini

1) Wash and slice the zucchini and cut into 3/8" slices and throw away the ends. Steam zucchini over boiling water for a few minutes.

2) Arrange the zucchini on your food dehydrator trays, making sure the zucchini slices don't overlap.

3) Turn on your food dehydrator and set the temperature between 125°F and 135°F (or per your food dehydrator's instructions).

Dehydrated zucchini will be brittle when fully dried.

Drying time: between 5-11 hours.

Please remember to rotate your trays for even drying.

37
DEHYDRATING COOKED MEAT

Meat, it's what's for dinner! :-)

Dehydrating meat that is pre-cooked and pre-sliced – gives us the perfect way for dehydrating meat safely!... Let's make lots of great stews and soups with it! I don't teach you how to make Jerky in this book; you'll find instructions for that either in your food dehydrator owner's manual, or simply do a search on your PC for "how to make beef jerky" and you'll find tons of ideas!

Meats are the building block of proteins for the body, and it's so easy to have your own dehydrated meats on hand. Meats can be dehydrated by smoke, freeze-dried, or cured by salt. But we're all about the 'easy' here as in 'easy'-food-dehydrating!

So for example, when preparing chicken for the family dinner, put some extra chicken in the cooking pot and save it to dehydrate later on!

Or as my brother says, "I'm saving it for Ron" –
"late...R on"!

So let's get some cooked meat dehydrated NOW before inflation hits big time – and meat prices rise even more!

Dehydrating cooked meat is VERY easy to do!

(Important: While vegetables re-hydrate very well, I personally cannot state the same for meats. You may experience a more chewy texture than you'd like… but on the other hand, it's better than not having ANY meat available at all to eat, that is, unless you're a vegetarian! Feel free to experiment with longer re-hydrating times for less-chewy meat!)

What's The Ideal Temperature To Use
for Dehydrating Cooked Meats?

Cooked meats are best dehydrated at 160°F - but please consult your food dehydrator's "owner manual" for their specific instructions.

Preparation for Dehydrating Cooked Meats

Your meat is already cooked, so that's one step saved - so no further preparation is necessary. The best meats to use are choice cuts -- the tender cuts - so they won't be chewy or tough.

**The less fat on the meat, the better -
as it's the fat in meat that causes the meat to go rancid.**

A great thing about using pre-sliced meats is that they are uniform in size, therefore they will all dehydrate at the same rate.

Dehydrated meats are perfect to use in stews, soups, or in a beef stroganoff for example. Make sure the meat pieces are SMALL and UNIFORM in size, if you didn't use pre-sliced meats, so they dehydrate and re-hydrate more evenly.

Vacuum sealed dehydrated cooked meats can last up to 2 to 3 weeks at room temperature. To maintain the quality of dehydrated meats, please refrigerate or store in the freezer until ready to use.

**Dehydrated meats will stay fresh
for up to six months
in the freezer --
without freezer burn!**

38
DEHYDRATING CHICKEN

When dehydrating chicken, use pre-cooked, pre-sliced chicken breast!

I decided to use my favorite sandwich meat in a tub: (yeah, I sometimes don't have time to stand in line at the deli!) Shown on the dehydrator trays below, are slices of pre-cooked Sliced Chicken Breast by Hillshire Farms.

The package filled four of my Nesco Dehydrator trays, with five slices on each tray, and it only took TWO hours to become fully dehydrated!

Don't forget to turn the heat UP to 160°F -- never dehydrate meat on a lower setting, that's not safe (germ-wise).

Dehydrated Chicken is Very E-A-S-Y to do!

Following are some photos of the sliced chicken on the dehydrator 'before' and 'after' dehydrating.

Ideal Temperature to Use
for Dehydrating Cooked Chicken:

Pre-cooked chicken is best dehydrated at 160°F as mentioned on the previous page - but please consult your food dehydrator's "owner manual" for their specific instructions.

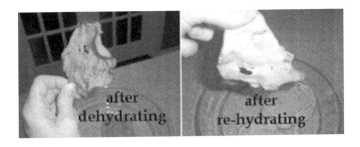

As you can see in the photo above, just look how crispy the chicken was after dehydrating! I then purposely draped a slice of the re-hydrated chicken around my finger so you could see that it was indeed moist again.

I also decided to make a small amount of chicken stock (from my favorite Better Than Bouillon by Superior Touch) and wow, what a difference that made to the re-hydrated chicken! *Make a note of that! :-)*

IMPORTANT: Re-hydrate in the refrigerator in
CLEAN water or the stock.
Don't leave it out on the counter top!
Don't let the chicken go 'off'!

Re-hydrate in Chicken Stock for Added Taste!

39
DEHYDRATING BEEF

Today, Dehydrating Beef was on my dehydrating to-do list. I find it hard to slice my own roast beef (I don't have an electric slicer), so I did the next best thing, bought the meat pre-sliced and pre-cooked!

Just like the sliced turkey (coming up), it dehydrated beautifully AND re-hydrated very well too! I used a 7 oz. plastic tub of Pre-Cooked Roast Beef from Target Stores. The Roast Beef tub from Target filled all four of my Nesco Dehydrator trays, with about three slices on each tray. TWO hours later, it was fully dehydrated!

Don't forget to turn the heat UP to 160°F -- never dehydrate meat on a lower setting, that's not safe (germ-wise).

And just like the chicken, I couldn't believe how simple it was to do! Here are some photos on the next page of the sliced roast beef on the dehydrator 'before' and 'after' dehydrating.

Ideal Temperature to Use
for Dehydrating Cooked Roast Beef:

Cooked roast beef is best dehydrated at 160°F as mentioned on the previous page - but please consult your food dehydrator's "owner manual" for their specific instructions.

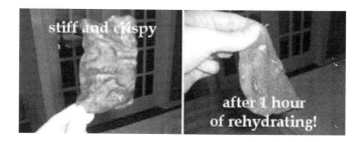

Shown above is a slice of roast beef held by its corner, to show you how stiff the roast beef was after dehydrating, and then I took another photo, just an hour later, of how limp the roast beef was after re-hydrating!

IMPORTANT: re-hydrate in the refrigerator in CLEAN water or beef STOCK.

Don't leave it out on the counter top and let the expensive roast beef go bad!

40
DEHYDRATING TURKEY

Dehydrating turkey that is pre-cooked and pre-sliced couldn't be easier! So off to the refrigerator I went and took out a 9 oz. plastic tub of Sliced Turkey I'd bought from Target Stores.

The package from Target filled all four of my Nesco Dehydrator trays, with around three slices of turkey on three trays, and four slices on the fourth... and I couldn't believe that it only took TWO hours to become fully dehydrated!

Don't forget to turn the heat UP to 160°F – never dehydrate meat on a lower setting, that's not safe (germ-wise).

Below are some photos of the sliced turkey on the dehydrator 'before' and 'after' dehydrating!

Ideal Temperature to Use
for Dehydrating Cooked Turkey:

Cooked turkey is best dehydrated at 160°F as mentioned on the previous page- but please consult your food dehydrator's "owner manual" for their specific instructions.

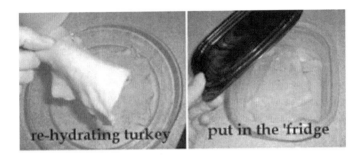

re-hydrating turkey | put in the 'fridge

As you can see in the photo above, I purposely draped a slice of the re-hydrated turkey around my finger so you could see that it was indeed moist again, i.e. not straight and crispy! I was very pleased with the results, to say the least.

IMPORTANT: re-hydrate in the refrigerator
in CLEAN water or STOCK.

Don't leave it out on the counter top!
Don't let the turkey go 'off'!

In the photo above, are three packages of pre-cooked turkey, all vacuum-sealed with their oxy-packs and ready to store. I will check on these in about a month, to make sure they haven't 'turned'... because there is fat in meat and we don't want to be eating rancid bad turkey!

UPDATE: The turkey is still 'perfectly good' after one month with no refrigeration!

41
DEHYDRATING PET FOOD

Make your own Feasts -- Fit For Fido and Fifi!
Chicken, Beef, and Pork Make Perfect Pet Treats

My husband and I were out swimming when we noticed this tiny dog on our patio, looking over at us.

Whenever we attempted to get close to her, she'd run off. It was about a month later, on my father's 80th birthday (as this book goes to press, it was over four years ago!), that the little doggie needed help – she had a huge tick on her ear which we immediately had removed! This time, she didn't run away and she gladly let us help her!

We drove around our local streets asking if anyone had a missing pooch - but no-one laid claim.

We then adopted this fantastic Miniature Pinscher, I decided right then and there that I would learn how to make my own doggie food for her!

Now, about once a month, usually on a Saturday morning for me, I get going, and it takes me about two hours from start to finish. I'd spend any amount of time, really, making this for my dog, as she's such a FANTASTIC loving pet! Turns out, she loves chicken, beef, and pork -- and I use a pressure cooker to prepare this for her.

Details on how to make this super doggie food is on the next page, and I want to add that you can make it from my dehydrated vegetables, AND it can be dehydrated AFTER it's made and then re-hydrated for doggie consumption!

Chicken Chow for Dogs

Our Min Pin's **FAVORITE** *Pet Food – Made with Love!*

Dog Food Chicken Chow Ingredients:

- 1/4 cup of millet and 1/4 cup of quinoa (rinsed in a fine sieve to remove the bitter taste)

- handful of whole wheat (or plain) egg noodles

- 1/4 cup of orzo

- six boneless, skinless chicken thighs or same amount of beef, or pork (save money by buying on sale and freezing)

followed by:

- 1 cup of chopped fresh carrots (or about a 1/2 cup dehydrated)

- 1/2 cup of sliced celery (two tablespoons dehydrated)

- 1 cup of sweet potato, diced (1/2 cup dehydrated)

- 1 cup of butternut squash, diced (1/2 cup dehydrated)

- 2 cups of chicken stock for the millet/quinoa/egg noodle/orzo and

- 2 cups of chicken stock for the chicken and vegetables in the pressure cooker

Note: Use vegetable stock* if you're substituting the chicken with beef, or pork as the chicken and vegetable stocks (by Superior Touch) do not contain onion - good news for dogs!

*I choose to use Better Than Bouillon stock by Superior Touch

Here's How You Make Chicken Chow Dog Food!

1) Put the (dehydrated) carrots, celery, sweet potato, and butternut squash aside in some boiling water in a measuring jug for about 5 minutes to re-hydrate then put in the pressure cooker. If using fresh veggies, simply place in the pressure cooker. Add two cups of chicken stock. Do not add salt or pepper. Make sure the stock you use is onion-free, because onions are poisonous to dogs.

2) Cook millet, quinoa, egg noodles, and orzo in a separate pan with 2 cups of chicken stock. Watch it to make sure it doesn't stick as it absorbs the stock rapidly! This takes about 20 minutes tops to cook. Add hot water to the mix if it dries out too soon. Keep an eye on it!

3) Place six boneless, skinless chicken thighs, (or similar amount of pork, or beef) -- on top of the veggies that are now in the pressure cooker. Make sure the meat pieces are of similar size for even cooking.

4) Cook according to your pressure cooker's directions. Mine only takes around 7 minutes! ... It's a Fagor. Almost felt like singing in Italian there ... ALMOST ... you know, when the moon hits your eye, like a big-a pizza pie - it's a Fagor! ... OK ... When the pressure cooking is done, remove the meat from the top and let it cool on a chopping board. When it's cooled, chop it into small bite-sized pieces.

5) Then add the vegetable contents from the pressure cooker to your pan of millet, quinoa, orzo, using a slotted spoon so that the majority of liquid (stock) is left behind ... you can add some of that stock later IF you think your mixture is too dry.

6) Add the chopped meat to the mix along with four teaspoons of the vitamin mix (see next page for the vitamin mix) and then portion it all out into six or seven containers with lids and then freeze them. Our Min Pin absolutely LOVES this dog food!

Adding Vitamins to
Homemade Dog Food for Good Health

As mentioned above, to the whole pan I've just made I add four teaspoons of this powder mixture (coming up) which are available in individual bottles at health food stores or online:

- 1/2 cup of Alfalfa (powder)

- 1 cup of Bone Meal (powder)

- 1 cup of Brewers Yeast (powder)

- 1/2 cup Kelp (powder)

Mix these four items together -- stir gently! I made a huge cloud in the kitchen the first time I stirred this over-ambitiously!!!

This vitamin batch lasts for about six- to nine months. I keep it in an airtight container (an old cool whip tub with the contents and quantities used written on the lid so I don't forget!)

My friend, Bev, wanted me to point out that we aren't dehydrating the dog food AFTER it's been made, rather we are USING dehydrated veggies to MAKE the dog food! -- Thanks Bev!

BUT, do you know, that's probably something to try... (dehydrating the chicken chow after it's made). UPDATE: I did try that – so see next page for the great results!

Here it is after re-hydrating it... with perfect results:

Make Your Own Doggie Biscuits

BY SHARON (IN TEXAS)

Ingredients:

- 1/2 cup millet

- 1/2 cup quinoa

- 3 cups chicken stock

- 2 large carrots, sliced

- 1 cup rolled oats

- 3 medium white potatoes, cubed

Here's how to make them!

1) Rinse the millet and quinoa under cold water for a minute or so.

2) Make the stock, and peel and dice the potatoes. Peel and slice the carrots.

3) Put all in a pan and bring to a boil, simmer for 15 minutes or until all is cooked – watch the pan as it can stick if you're not careful. It gets very thick.

4) Let it cool a bit and use a teaspoon to drop blobs onto your dehydrator (fruit roll) sheets and pat them down with the back of the spoon or use damp fingers – then they're not too tall to fit in between the dehydrator trays.

5) Let them really crust over, then use a blunt knife (I used a butter knife) to scrape them up off the fruit roll sheet, and then turned them over and dehydrated them some more until fully dried.

ready to flip over after first crusting-over

Instant doggie biscuits!

Sharon says: *"I used your idea of using millet and quinoa too – and thanks for letting me share this - Sharon."*

Note from Susan: They look just like chicken nuggets!!!

42
STORING
DEHYDRATED FOOD

When you're ready for storing your dehydrated food, it's important to pay attention to how you handle it before it's packed away.

Each of the items listed below are covered in more detail in their own chapters.

Wear Latex Gloves so that you don't transfer germs from your hands to the food. (There are latex-free gloves available if you're allergic to latex). I use these latex gloves more than once; I wash my hands while wearing them in the kitchen sink, dry them off on a clean towel, and then drape them over my dish draining rack -- so the latex gloves are ready for another use. We're almost ready for storing your dehydrated food! After a day or overnight of conditioning it's time to vacuum seal your fruits and vegetables!

Save Money by Food Vacuum Sealing and Storing Dehydrated Food for the Long-Term

It's important when food vacuum-sealing your fruit and vegetables that you have an 'oxypack' tucked inside your food vacuum-sealer bag or jar. These little oxygen packs absorb oxygen and are readily available in different sizes, such as the 100cc, 300cc, and up. The reason for different sized oxygen packs depends upon what size container your dehydrated foods will be placed in.

Storing Dehydrated Food in Mylar Bags

If you're going to store your vacuum-packed foods in Mylar bags, first thing to do is vacuum seal your dehydrated fruits and vegetables in the food vacuum sealer bags. Then they are stored in the Mylar bags, with NO air removal necessary from the Mylar bags, as the air has already been vacuumed out when you created the vacuum-sealed bags with the oxypacks in them.

For storing your dehydrated fruit and vegetables for daily or weekly use, try using different sized airtight mason jars which sit very nicely on your upper kitchen cabinet shelves. Those are my mason jars in my kitchen on the cover of this book! There are ready-made food vacuum sealer bags – and there are food-vacuum-sealer-rolls available to make the perfect-length-bag to suit!

Bags, Bins, and Buckets for Storing Dehydrated Food

Next, I choose to wrap up my vacuum-packed packages with cheap plastic wrap, to keep sharp edges from puncturing other packets – and then they go into the Mylar bags along with a 300cc oxygen pack.

Mylar bags are made from a silvery-grey polyester film and are very shiny in appearance; they are very tough and tear-resistant and are ideal for long-term food packaging. They provide an extra layer of protection to our individual food packets. And for final storage in a garage, for instance, you can then put the Mylar bags in plastic lidded bins or feed buckets with lids. Easy to move, water-proof, bug-proof, and air-tight!

Use Latex Gloves and Keep Germs at Bay

Use Latex Gloves when handling your dehydrated foods, because there's no point in ruining your dehydrated fruits and veggies by soiling your food with 'dirty' hands.

It takes no time at all to slip on a pair of gloves... no, not those boxing gloves... but a pair of latex gloves!

There are many sources of gloves: they can be found on the shelves of your local supermarket, in drugstores, and online – I get mine from my local grocery store and/or Amazon.com. Use latex-free gloves, also known as vinyl gloves, if you're allergic to latex.

I use the vinyl variety all the time, but not because I'm allergic to latex, but because there's no powdery-stuff left on your hands... nice feature!

What I have also noticed while wearing them is it makes it much easier to smooth out frozen peas or corn on your dehydrator tray's mesh sheets. The warmth of your hands don't melt the peas or corn as fast because you're wearing them and it provides a barrier which slows down the heat transference and it stops the frozen peas/corn from sticking to your fingers! It's very easy to break up clumps too when you wear them.

When I've finished using them, I'll wash and rinse them off while I'm still wearing them, and then let them air dry on the dish drainer, so I can use them again!

"Waste not, want not"... as the old saying goes...

43
CONDITIONING
FRUITS AND VEGETABLES
AFTER DEHYDRATING

Conditioning fruits and vegetables is simply the act of letting your dehydrated goodies cool down, and then putting them into zip-lock bags and letting them hang around your kitchen for a day or overnight.

When the dehydrated fruit and vegetables are done, I transfer them to a dish (or two), which I just let sit and cool down on the kitchen counter. You can simply leave them on the dehydrator trays, but sometimes you forget they're still in there -- hence my using bowls on the kitchen counter-top!

When they are totally cooled off, I put them into the zip-lock freezer-type bags. Sandwich-style bags are not strong enough and can easily have your dehydrated foods poke through and puncture the bag!

Feel free to re-use the freezer bags because they're not cheap -- I throw them away when I see any sticky residue left behind. I use some bags specifically for fruit and I use my black felt-tipped pen to mark the bags as 'fruit only', and have some bags just for vegetables.

NOTE:

I will never re-use a plastic bag that has had meat in it

Drying Out Fruit and Vegetables – AKA "Conditioning"

This drying-out time lets the 'more moist'* foods spread their moisture around to the drier pieces! This process is called 'conditioning'.

*(Is there such a word as 'moister'?) ☺

If your fruits or veggies are still sticking together a bit too much in the zip-lock bag, simply place the dehydrated food back in the dehydrator for an hour or so, and then let it cool off again.

Then put the dried food back in the bag(s) again for a couple of hours. They're now ready for vacuum sealing! Mushrooms are well-known for needing a second go around on the dehydrator! Some foods will remain sticky, though, such as dehydrated plums (prunes).

The photo below some Elephant Garlic conditioning in a zip-lock bag.

44
OXYGEN ABSORBER PACKS

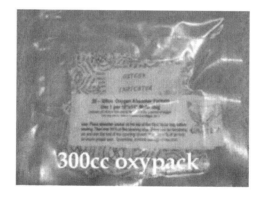

Oxygen Packs are life support for Jars, Bags, Buckets, and Bins! It's important to use oxygen packs, or oxygen absorbers as they're also known, when vacuum-sealing your fruit and vegetables after dehydrating and conditioning. Tuck it inside the vacuum bag just before vacuuming, or drop one in the mason jar just before screwing on its lid.

Why Use Them?

The oxygen absorbers protect dry foods from insect damage and extend the shelf-life by preventing mold growth which eliminates the need for additives like BHA, BHT, and sorbates, etc. The oxygen packs are non-toxic, which is good to know, as they are in direct-contact with our food!

These little oxygen absorbers are readily available in different sizes, such as the 100cc, 300cc, and 2000cc. Pick them up at Amazon.com. The reason for different sizes depends upon what size container your dehydrated foods are placed in.

For a quart-sized mason jar or vacuum bag, use a 100cc oxy-pack (shown just below and on the next two pages). For a 10" x 14" Mylar bag, use a 300cc oxy-pack (shown above). For storage bins or buckets, use 2000cc oxy-pack.

Blue/Purple Pill = Bad ----- Pink Pill = Good!

When the 100-pack of oxy-packs first arrives, BEFORE OPENING IT or putting it away, I'll immediately check for the little pill in the bag. It MUST BE PINK. If it's BLUE/PURPLE... that's not good.

It turns BLUE/PURPLE when the pill has absorbed oxygen, therefore telling you that the contents of the shipment are probably no-good. So before you OPEN that shipped package, check for a pink pill. If it's blue/purple, return that shipment unopened for a replacement order!

If the pill is good, I'll open the new 100-pack bag, and take out 5 quart-size vacuum-sealer bags. Place 20 oxy-packs from the 100-pack bag into the quart-size vacuum-sealer bags, and immediately vacuum seal them. So I now have five quart-size bags with 20 oxy-packs in each of them. The pink pill from the original bag can go into one of the five bags -- no need to throw it away, we can use it up!

The reason for doing this is because I don't want to continually open and seal the same bag to take out one or two oxy-packs, it would soon ruin the other oxy-packs with air infiltration before we even get a chance to use them!

Cut Just Below the Old Seal

When I'm ready to use an oxygen pack, I simply cut along the bottom of the seal at the top of the bag (as straight as you can and as close to the old seal as you can, see photo below) -- then remove as many packets as I need and put them in the dehydrated food bags that are waiting to be vacuum sealed.

Reseal Opened Oxy-Pack Bags
Immediately After Use

Then straight away, I'll re-vacuum and seal the oxy-pack bag (see photo next page). I can re-seal an oxy-pack bag about four times ... and if I've any remaining packets and the bag gets 'too short' to reseal, I'll put those remaining packets into a new bag and vacuum seal it!

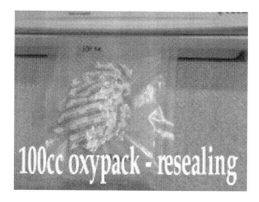

45
MASON JARS

Ideal storage for dehydrated food! I love to use mason jars to store my dehydrated fruit and vegetables! They are airtight -- and can be easily kept on your pantry shelves in the kitchen, and behind closed doors, which keeps direct light off them also, which is a good thing!

I use air-tight mason jars for every-day use -- when I'm ready to make a quick soup, or need to add some dehydrated vegetables to a recipe, I can quickly add some dehydrated vegetables without having to mess around preparing fresh vegetables.

(Don't get me wrong, I'll take fresh vegetables over dehydrated any day, but we're all about doing this for long-term storage).

By keeping the dehydrated vegetables in the jars, it means I'm not opening up my Mylar bags all the time to retrieve a vacuumed packet and having to re-seal the Mylar bag afterward.

Mason jars look great on your shelves! Impress your friends and family!

You can use smaller air-tight jars for items that you don't use a lot of, such as garlic, and spices. I like the fact that they are made of glass; not only can you see the contents in the jar, you can see at a glance how much is left!

When you're ready to refill your jars from your stock, just go pick out one from your stash of stored Mylar bags. Open it, take out a packet (or two) and reseal the Mylar bag, and refill your jar!

Do not forget to sterilize your mason jars before use.

It Can't Get Much Easier Than This!

We also need to have a 100cc oxypack in the jar, and an easy way to tell if the oxypack is 'worn out' is when you take the lid off... If the lid opens without a popping sound, you will need to replace the old pack with a new one.

NOTE: I'll keep the 'old' 100cc oxypack and put that in the smaller jars (the jars I use for the elephant garlic and spices). Even though they may not have much 'life' left in the old oxypacks, there's probably enough life left in them for the small jars!

When doing the above suggestion, take out the old packet and toss it; that way you won't end up with a jar full of oxypacks and not know which one was the 'last one in'!

46
VACUUM SEALER BAGS

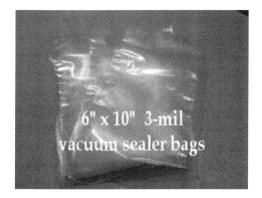

Now you're ready for sealing and storing your dehydrated food!

Vacuum bags for food storage and sealing can be purchased in varying sizes and thicknesses… so make sure you purchase ones that are at least 3-mil thick. Any thinner and you may have some brittle foods puncturing your bags after the vacuuming! And we don't want that to happen.

The size I personally use are 6" x 10" and following is the link to their site and the name of the company is DC Processing Equipment http://www.dcprocessingequipment.com/store-products-30-0106-W-WS-Vacuum-Sealer-Bags---6%94-x-10%94-%96-100-Bags_1095524379.html

Apologies for such a long URL above! Or try this: Google DC Processing Equipment, or just go to their site by typing in: www.dcprocessingequipment.com and look there for their bags!

~*~

Look closely at your bag: One side of the bag is smooth, and the other side is 'textured'. This is to enable the food-vacuum-sealer to draw the air out. And no, it doesn't matter which side up they go on the vacuum sealer machine! This was brought to my attention by my Realtor-friend, Bev Miller, who was trying so hard to vacuum her Mylar bags when she discovered that it won't work because the Mylar bags' surface is SMOOTH! She's so smart!

NOTE:
We don't VACUUM the Mylar bags,
but we DO use the sealing element
of the Food Sealer machine to seal the Mylar bags

You need the textured side on the food vacuum sealer bags to let the air out! You learn something new every day!

The food vacuum sealer bags we use are ordered over the internet and shipped right to our door. Use the link provided above which will take you to DC Processing where I buy my bags, or you can of course purchase them in your local superstore – just make sure they're 3-mil thick!

Canning Funnel to the Rescue!

To aid in filling the bags, I use a canning funnel. They are relatively inexpensive and come in very handy whether you are filling your plastic vacuum bags or the mason jars. See these photos, below, showing how to do it! With a bit of practice you'll soon have it down pat!

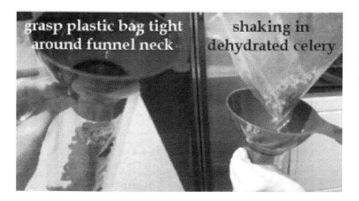

NOTE: After vacuuming our bags, I pull out a 2ft length (approx.) of plastic wrap. I then wrap the vacuum-sealed package in it! I have a pictorial on how to wrap the packages too, coming up soon, pg 160).

47
VACUUM SEALER ROLLS

Vacuum Sealer Rolls are super for making "just the right size" bags! Food sealer vacuum rolls can be purchased in varying lengths, and widths so make sure you don't get ones that are too wide for your particular machine...

They make it very convenient when you have long-length foods that you want to store, such as spaghetti! No need to break the spaghetti in half to store! In fact, I left the spaghetti in its box.., just in case I forget how long to cook it!

NOTE:
I have noticed the white printed section
(for you to write the bag's contents on)
tends to 'come off' and stick to the
lower heating element strip and
the upper roller on the food sealer machine.

Don't worry, this white residue wipes off very easily with a clean damp cloth. I wipe it down immediately when I see the white powdery-stuff on the strip -- so it doesn't hamper future bag sealings. It's good practice, anyway, to keep your roller and strip clean. You'll create a tight seal, and that's definitely what we're aiming for.

How to Create Your Own Bags

1) Cut off the desired length of bag at right angles, i.e. cut it STRAIGHT across at 90 degrees. If you keep the cut straight you'll have an easier time vacuuming it, not only that, you'll have rectangular bags and not odd misshapen-parallelogram bags!

2) Seal one end. Then add your food to be vacuumed, flatten the package as best you can. Don't forget to add an oxygen absorber!

3) Vacuum and then seal the custom-length bag! Write the contents on it too, and the date.

NOTE:
After vacuuming our bags, I pull out a 2ft length (approx.) of plastic wrap. I then wrap the package in it! (pg 160).

Another good reason to use plastic wrap is if a vacuumed-bag seal gives way during storage, then the plastic wrap acts as an extra air- and water-tight layer! My real reason for using plastic wrap is to keep the bags from accidentally puncturing each other in the first place, when you are putting them in the Mylar bags for long-term storage.

48
MYLAR BAGS

The next-to-last destination of your pint- or quart sized-vacuum bags can be Mylar bags. (The final step is the plastic lidded bins, or buckets, coming up on pages 153 and 155).

These special Mylar bags are made from a polyester film and are very shiny in appearance; they are very tough and tear-resistant and are ideal for food packaging - it gives an extra layer of protection to our individual food packets that you'll place inside for safekeeping. The bags also keep the light and air out, when sealed properly, and are easy to write on with a black felt-tipped pen/marker!

The reason you can't vacuum these bags, (or is at least VERY hard to do) is that both sides of the bag are smooth. Take a close look at the plastic vacuum bags that the dehydrated food goes into first; you'll notice that one side is smooth and the other side is 'bumpy', for want of a better word. These textured 'bumps' enable the air to actually be drawn out of the bag, otherwise the two smooth surfaces just simply clamp shut tight together!

When you've filled your 10 inch x 14 inch bags, use a black felt tipped pen as mentioned above, to describe the contents of the bags and write the date on it too! I can get at least three plastic-wrap vacuum-packed packages into one bag, sometimes four. Don't overstuff. If you try to get more in, it makes it harder to seal the bag, plus you risk puncturing the vacuum-sealed packages inside, when one pokes against the other. That's the reason why I plastic-wrap the packages after vacuum sealing.

For a 10 inch by 14 inch bag, a 300cc oxypack is used.

NOTE: To make sure you understand -- we do not vacuum the Mylar bags, we only use the sealing function on the vacuum-sealer machine; *not the air removal function.*

The vacuum AND sealing takes place only on the food vacuum-sealer bags, or the food vacuum-sealer rolls.

Here Are Some Filled Mylar Bags, (see photos, below) Ready for Long-Term food Storage.

Inside you'll find three or four individually vacuum-sealed packages of say, peas. Each packet of peas are wrapped in plastic wrap to keep the pointy corners from puncturing its neighboring bag...

49
PLASTIC LIDDED BINS

Plastic lidded bins make great food stackers!

Consider using plastic lidded bins for easy closet, walk-in pantry, or garage storage, of dehydrated foods -- for long-term storage. It's better if you can find stack-able bins that you can't see through as it helps to keep the light out. Remember to write the contents on the bin's side and put the date on the bags that go in the bins!

PLEASE NOTE: This bin shown above is NOT airtight, i.e. some air can get in around the handles -- so it's pointless using the 2000cc oxygen absorber in these types of bins. Also note that we are using these large oxy packs IN ADDITION to the 100cc oxypacks that are already IN our sealed packages.

There are plastic lidded bins available that have snap-on lids that are truly airtight - like bucket lids - so use the 2000cc oxypack with those types of storage bins. Remember, these are NOT going to be opened on a regular basis, maybe twice a year or so, as we use up and rotate our stock.

When it came time to build my food storage wall,
I made sure that there was enough room between
the shelves 'height-wise' to fit the bins.
More on the storage wall in an upcoming chapter.

It's easy to change the factory-set shelf heights; simply drill new holes in the uprights! Use a nail and hammer to make a 'starter dimple/hole' in the uprights, so that your drill-bit doesn't wander when you first start drilling. Make sure you're using a drill bit that's suitable for metal, too.

Consider buying deep(er) shelving units so you can store your bins with the narrow side facing out, rather than the wide side facing out like I did. You'll be able to store more bins that way.

You're always wiser after the event!

50
FEED BUCKETS WITH LIDS

Feed buckets – not just for animals anymore!

Just like their lidded-bins counterparts, these 5-gallon #2 plastic food grade feed buckets with lids are fantastic for long-term storage of your dehydrated foods.

These can easily be stored in a closet, walk-in pantry, or your garage. These feed buckets with lids are readily available at your home building center or farm feed supply stores.

When you have your buckets filled with your Mylar bags which should have their contents and the date written on the bags, it's time to do the same on the outside of the bucket and date it!

Don't forget to add a 2000cc oxypack!
Remember, the dehydrated foods are being stored long-term, so we need to bear in mind that we don't want to be opening and closing these buckets on a daily basis -- ideally maybe twice a year, for stock rotation.

These buckets are great for stacking in the garage - preferably an air-conditioned garage...

NOTE: I came across some great Gamma2 lids at Amazon.com Apparently you 'hammer-on' the 'rim' and then you can simply screw-out the center part! One reviewer said it kept her flour etc. totally bug-free -- as they really are air-tight!

No more losing finger nails and hurting your finger tips trying to pry lids off, especially in cold weather... ouch!

We also have grey buckets from our favorite home improvement store and those cost slightly less than the white ones shown...

You can see the grey buckets in our Great Wall of Dehydrated Food photo and page coming up next!

51
DEHYDRATED FOOD
STORAGE WALL

When it's time to create more storage space for your buckets or bins, and boxes... check out my great wall of storage that started with a blank wall (well, I took some artwork down and moved a chair first!)

My husband went to the local hardware store and purchased two of the cheapest closet organizers that span 5' to 8' width and two extra 48" wire shelves. Turns out I still need some extra shelf-supporting clips, but they're on their way! If you don't have such a helpful-hubby (or wife!), then by all means, shop online and have it delivered! See the Closet Maid system(s) at Amazon.com

It's not very hard to do, just follow the instructions that are included in the closet shipping boxes. From start to finish, it took about three hours to do the whole job, see photo below!

I do intend to have some drapery on a rod for the dehydrated food storage wall, so that the whole shelving unit can be hidden behind it.

I may have another row of shelves right on top as there's still enough room left on the four uprights to do that but I'm not sure if I'll be able to access it...

But right now I'm worn out, so maybe tomorrow! I just wanted to share this with you all to give you an idea of what you can do at your home.

Total cost so far: $70
(not including food and buckets!!!)...

And I'm SURE I've got some drapes up in the attic...

Yessss! I found the drapes!...

Well look here - I finally finished the wall - it only took me around six months to get "a round tuit"!!!

I simply used an old curtain rod and wired it up to the top of the shelving's upright posts (drilled a hole in the tops first for the wire). I then sewed curtain rings on the backs of the curtain.

We all agree it certainly looks much better than seeing buckets, bins, and boxes!

52
PLASTIC WRAP
GUIDE

Here's a quick pictorial (see large photo next page) -- an easy plastic wrap guide -- your dehydrated fruit and vegetables can have this optional plastic wrap protection - easy to do as shown in the eight photographs!

step 1 - Fold excess vacuum bag top underneath

step 2 - Pull out 2 ft approx. plastic wrap. Place folded package down with the bag's fold facing the newly torn wrap edge (that's on your left)

step 3 - Fold the wrap over the top

step 4 - And continue folding/wrapping the package to your right

step 5 - Fold excess 'wings' see dotted line!

step 6 - From bottom upwards...

step 7 - ...and fold the top wing down

step 8 - Turn your package over so you can see your hand-written contents on vacuum bag through the wrap!

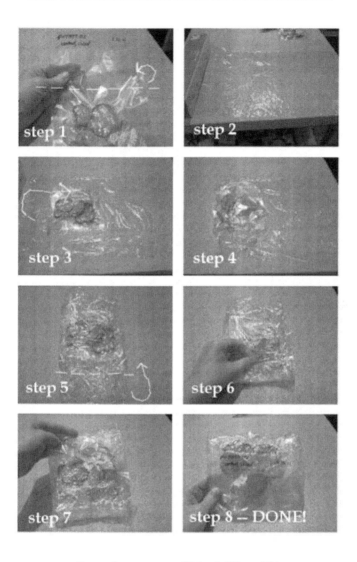

Dare I now say, "It's A Wrap"?!

NOTE: When you have taken out a packet of dehydrated food to use, don't throw away the plastic wrap! Instead, wrap it around an old cardboard paper-towel roll tube or fold the plastic wrap gently -- and USE IT AGAIN!

Why are we doing all this?

When you have dehydrated your food, it can become brittle and pretty sharp. Always use good quality vacuum bags and I've given you a good supplier (read the chapter on vacuum bags). To prevent the dehydrated food packets from puncturing the bag that's next to it in the Mylar bag, wrap the vacuumed bag first with plastic wrap, and follow this plastic wrap guide, on the previous page!

Recap: The sequence is to

1) Dehydrate the food.

2) Vacuum seal it with a 100cc oxypack tucked in the bag.

3) Wrap the package in plastic wrap to soften the corners to avoid puncturing other bags.

4) Put those packages in the Mylar bags along with a 300cc oxypack in the Mylar bag. Seal the Mylar bag, and write on it the bag's contents, and the date.

5) Lastly, put these Mylar bags in the bins and buckets with a 2000cc oxypack. When you add the 2000cc oxypacks, be aware that this is for LONG-TERM storage, i.e. you won't be opening up these bins often. Maybe 3 or 4 times per year.

53
FOOD DEHYDRATORS

What Are They and How Do They Work?

Food Dehydrators have been around for a very long time; when I first saw them about ten years ago I thought they were pretty much a passing fad and who on earth would want one of those?

But it wasn't through kitchen-gadget ads on TV or online that made me take the plunge -- it was due to the very real possibility of a world-wide food shortage in the next 20 years or so.

If you read up on super-power China, and about how much US debt they own, and how China must sustain a double-digit growth rate... it becomes obvious that to sustain a country that has four times the number of citizens than the US, there needs to be enough food in the world to feed China... and the rest of the world.

But, that's Twenty Years Away you say...

The reason I'm preparing NOW is because of the threat of inflation -- or even possibly hyper-inflation. Every time more money is printed by our government, it dilutes the buying power of the dollars that are already in circulation.

It takes MORE of your dollars in your wallet to buy things now than it did six months ago. Who knows what the food prices will be six months from now? It all sounds a bit scary?

Yep. BUT, if the people predicting all this are right... I'll gladly start putting food away NOW, here and there, if/when it goes on sale -- before inflation sky-rockets -- take it home, dehydrate it, and store it!

So Let's Get Some Food PUT AWAY Right Now!

If the people predicting all this are wrong? I'd rather look silly later on, than be starving later on. This way, we can help out friends and relatives who did not prepare and thought that food-shortages in the USA just could not possibly happen!

So – How Do Food Dehydrators Work?

Food dehydrators work by simply removing the moisture in foods by means of an air-circulating fan and a heating element. They have temperature controls ranging from 90°F to 160°F so you can choose the appropriate setting. They are not silent-running -- but they do pretty much run in the background. In fact, they create a good white-noise! Beats hearing the neighbor's barking dogs and street noise!

The dehydrators for home use are lightweight - so they're easily portable. The two I own are made from plastic. One is black with molded panels that resemble leather-hide. The other model is a speckled white/gray sturdy plastic.

One dehydrator has its fan in the rear and the other model has its fan at the top in the lid.

Foods Can Be Preserved in Other Ways

Foods can be preserved by canning, freeze-drying, smoking, or DEHYDRATING. To me, the easiest method by far is dehydrating!

The simplicity of it appealed to me more than anything.

I have two dehydrators below for you to check out: Excalibur and NESCO Dehydrators coming right up

EXCALIBUR Food Dehydrator

Here's the EXCALIBUR Dehydrator, featuring Pull-out Trays and Rear Fans. The EXCALIBUR food dehydrator company has been in business making dehydrators for over thirty years! They offer four-tray starter models all the way up to nine-tray models, and they make Commercial dehydrators too.

This EXCALIBUR dehydrator four-model tray offers no on/off switch. Higher grade EXCALIBUR food dehydrator models DO have an on/off switch! These dehydrators are the only dehydrators with the unique Parallexx Horizontal Airflow Drying System. This basically means that the circulating fan is at the rear.

The larger capacity you go with EXCALIBUR dehydrators, the larger the circulating fan and wattage. And the more food you'll be able to dehydrate in one sitting! The plastic exterior body of the dehydrator is molded to look like leather (I think!)...

EXCALIBUR dehydrators have their temperature selector on the top. It's easy to read and use.

These dehydrators have trays that pull out from the front, like a chest of drawers. You simply slide up the front panel to take it out of the dehydrator for easy access to the trays. I have found the pull-out trays to be a real handy feature/bonus of the EXCALIBUR dehydrator as you can proof your bread dough, by taking out the top trays and just leaving in the bottom tray!

NOTE: Don't try proofing bread in a four-tray dehydrator model, there's not enough height to the unit -- unless you're doing hot-dog-type buns; use a 9-tray model for proofing loaves of bread.

Simply set the dehydrator temperature to 115°F and let it warm up. Place a shallow pan of water on the very bottom and put one tray directly above it with the bowl of dough placed on that tray. Cover your dough with a cloth to keep it from drying out! Let it sit for up to an hour -- whatever your bread recipe calls for!

Rotate the Trays

I have noticed that the trays in the middle dry faster, so, like the other Nesco dehydrator (discussed next), I rotate these trays too! Not only from top to bottom etc., but also turn the dehydrator trays 180 degrees as the fan is located at the back of the machine and obviously dries out food faster that are closest to the fan.

The EXCALIBUR dehydrator company offers Spices and Jerky supplies, along with Books, and Raw & Living Food Helpers. You can also purchase ParaFlexx non-stick Drying Sheets for making fruit roll ups!

NESCO Food Dehydrator

Here's the NESCO Dehydrator, featuring Stackable Trays with the Fan located in the Lid. The NESCO dehydrator company has been making food dehydrators for over thirty years and their patented food dehydrators feature technology that dries your food faster and evenly.

According to NESCO, you get even-drying from top to bottom due to NESCO's Converge-A-Flow® air-flow design. (**This is supposed to eliminate the tray rotation, but I still rotate the trays anyway**). Nesco makes clear food dehydrator trays so you can see what's drying... and they also have a Snackmaster® Square Dehydrator and Jerky Maker.

The dehydrator fan is located on the top in the lid, (which is better than some models where the fan is at the bottom, as it makes it a breeze to keep clean!)

There isn't an on/off switch on the NESCO dehydrator, you just have to plug the dehydrator in, and unplug it when you're done. You can buy a 'timer-switch' from hardware stores IF you want to have the luxury of the NESCO dehydrator turning off, say after ten hours, if you know you won't be home to shut it off!

The NESCO food dehydrator models have a temperature selector which is located on the lid and is easy to read and use. A neat feature of these NESCO dehydrators is that you can stack as many trays as you want, within reason!

I feel good about being able to use as many dehydrator trays as needed, rather than having to run the machine with empty trays (like the Excalibur model)... Sometimes I'll have just four trays going, and some days, seven!

I began with the NESCO four-tray model, and purchased additional trays, they come in sets of two at a very reasonable price. I was pleased to see that the new NESCO dehydrator trays color-matched perfectly with the old(er) trays for a seamless stacking experience!

NOTE: NESCO® states you must use a minimum of four trays whether you've got food on all four trays or not, for the fan to create even-drying of the food.

The only time I ever need to run the dehydrator with less than four trays is when I make fruit roll ups -- I only have two Fruit Roll Sheets that came with the dehydrator so only two trays are actually being used! So, when only using TWO trays for the roll ups, I'll add an empty tray (without the clean-a-Screens, see info. below) in-between the fruit roll trays and one more on top, so that I have the four tray minimum for drying.

NESCO dehydrators also have "Clean-a-Screens" which are circular plastic mesh flexible screens. They have little half-round cutouts for your fingers to enable easy removal of the sheets -- and that's great!

They fit neatly into the dehydrator trays and this enables you to keep small foods from falling through to the trays below (as foods shrink when they dry out!)

Also, any sticky fruits/foods clean off really easily from these dehydrator screens - which is their intended purpose.

My 4-tray model came complete with two Fruit Roll Sheets as mentioned above, and these are like the Clean-a-Screens inasmuch as they fit neatly into the trays, but these are solid so that the tray's contents CAN'T spill or seep through! *Important when pouring puréed fruits to make the fruit roll-ups!*

The NESCO dehydrator company also offers cookbooks and Jerky Gun Kits.

54
VACUUM SEALERS

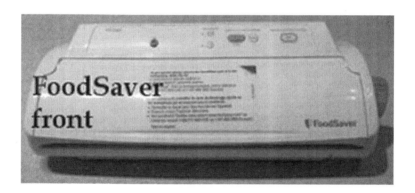

The FoodSaver® V2240 is great!

When we have dehydrated our foods, we let it condition.

After conditioning, our next step
is to place the foods into the
quart-size or pint-size vacuum bags.

Add the 100cc oxy-pack, and now we're ready to use the FoodSaver machine which vacuums the air out of our bags. In order to preserve foods properly for long-term storage, it is very important to keep out these three elements: moisture, air, and light.

By dehydrating the food first, that takes care of the 'moisture' issue. Second, by vacuuming the bags, we achieve the 'air' removal. Finally, by storing our vacuum-sealed food in Mylar bags and then in bins, preferably in a dark area, that takes care of the 'light' issue. We now have food on hand, put away for long-term storage and safe-keeping.

Compact, Lightweight: Does the Job Well

It's very easy to use and you can vacuum either 'wet' or 'dry' foods. The machine automatically defaults to the 'dry' setting which is handy for us because that's all we're vacuuming!

IMPORTANT:

For proper vacuum-bag placement, please look at the following photos and explanations.

The photos show you exactly where to place the open end of the bag on the machine for perfect seals every time!

Correct Placement of Your Bags on the Vacuum Sealer

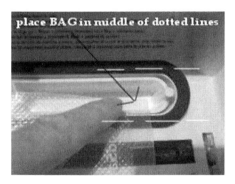

The photo above shows you WHERE TO PLACE the cut EDGE of your vacuum sealer bag. The edge of the bag goes right in the center of the black vacuum channel, shown by my two white dashed lines.

Hold the bag in place with your hands away from the area, then close the lid.

Press the lever down that's on the right side of the machine. This holds the bag in place (see photo next page).

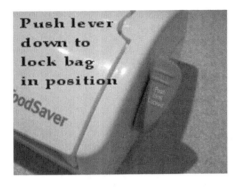

While the bag is clamped, I smooth out the contents of the bag, making it pretty flat. This makes it much easier to store in the Mylar bags. Now, simply press the <u>dark</u> "vacuum and seal" button. (See photo below, the dark button is on the left). You'll now experience the air being drawn out of the bag, and this lasts about 6-10 seconds!

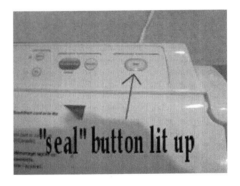

When the vacuuming is finished, you'll see the machine switch over to the "seal" mode -- and the seal button will light up in red as **shown by the arrow** in the photo above. Let the machine seal the bag and be patient! This takes about 6 seconds. When you see the light go off, you can now raise the handle which locks the lid in place, and lift the lid and retrieve the vacuumed and sealed bag!

NOTE:
There are times when we do <u>not</u> need to use the vacuum feature such as when we are just <u>sealing</u> our Mylar bags.

Simply place the edge of your **Mylar bag** beyond the first dark strip - - about an inch is good.

Take a look at the 'open wide' photo (above) and you'll see the dark **rectangular strip** in front of the oval vacuum-sealer channel. The strip heats up and when the lid is down, the roller in the lid holds the bag in close contact with the dark strip and makes the seal.

Just press the SEAL button this time, and your Mylar bag will be sealed without any vacuuming taking place! When you're vacuuming and sealing a few bags one after the other, please wait 20 seconds between each sealing to allow the strip to cool down before re-use!

I use a black felt-tipped pen and spend this 'waiting time' writing the bag's contents and the date on the very top of the bag (above the seal) that I've just vacuumed.

The photos above are showing the vacuum-sealer bags being vacuumed. This package will feel quite hard when it's been properly vacuum-sealed.

Try to pat the contents FLAT first before vacuum-sealing so that it's easier to pack the packages in the Mylar bags!

NOW we take these packages, (probably 3 or 4 packages) and put them in the Mylar bags, along with a 300cc oxypack, and SEAL the Mylar bag, i.e. NO vacuum function on the Mylar bags!

55
RE-HYDRATING FOOD:
HERE'S THE "BEFORE & AFTERS"!

Hopefully you've learned a lot about how to dehydrate your foods, so now it's time to:

put the water back in
and re-hydrate the food!

For a cupful of dehydrated veggies, for instance, I'll add water to the 2 cup mark in a glass measuring jug. In other words, add twice the amount of water to the amount of food you are re-hydrating. It's really only a case of making sure there's enough water for the foods to drink up, so keep your eye on it and add more water if it looks like it'll dry up before your foods are nice and plump again!

These dehydrated vegetables, in the photo on the next page, are from previously frozen bags of crinkle-cut carrots, peas, green beans, and some Ore-Ida Hash Brown potatoes -- along with dehydrated fresh onion, celery and elephant garlic!

Note:
What you see above is the humble/great beginnings
of a very tasty Vegetable Soup (see Recipes Section).

Check out the photo below where the water is being absorbed and you can see just how far up the jar the vegetables in the water have reached!

Should I Use Hot or Cold Water?

I'll use hot (boiling) water for re-hydrating food when I'm making a recipe that calls for hot 'stock' because my bouillon dissolves better in just-boiled water -- but if you know it'll be sitting around a while before you get to use it, then cold (clean) water works fine.

I must make an important point here: If you're re-hydrating food in hot water, please make sure to BRING IT BACK TO A BOIL while you're preparing your recipe.

You don't want to have food sitting around in hot/warm water without boiling it again -- be safe -- don't let any airborne germs get a chance to fester in it prior to eating!

It takes about an hour for small veggies to plump back up in the water; the larger veggies take longer, about two hours. Also note that you may want to cook your re-hydrated veggies a little longer than usual... it helps makes the vegetables taste like whole vegetables again.

carrots BEFORE

Water Quality Counts

Remember, the quality of the water you use while re-hydrating food IS important, as the water is being absorbed by the foods that you are going to eat re-hydrated again -- so don't skimp here by using nasty water! By nasty, you know what I mean! If you wouldn't drink it, don't use it! Make sure it's good, clean, drinking water.

It's not always necessary to re-hydrate your foods. For instance, you may want to grind up some of your dehydrated garlic to make garlic powder and grind up some dehydrated onions too for onion powder! Don't forget dehydrated celery for celery powder (add a little salt for celery salt).

If you're making a soup where the vegetables aren't sautéed in olive oil at the start of the recipe, then go ahead and just add them to the water, (or soup stock or soup base according to the recipe) in their dehydrated form! For the most part, they'll plump right up in the water/stock base if you let them sit and cook long enough!

Nutrients

Melba, a good friend of mine, asked me if dehydrated foods lose their nutritional value and how did they really taste when re-hydrated? I assured her that for the most part, they retain much of their nutritional value because all that's been taken out is the excess water during the dehydration process... (but like ALL fruits and vegetables, when cooked-to-death, they WILL lose nutrients!)

And the Taste?

I will admit that my first effort at re-hydrating carrots yielded somewhat spongy carrots, but when I cooked them a little more, they were fine. They were whole baby carrots and that might have had something to do with the sponginess... My sliced carrots re-hydrated perfectly! All the other vegetables just come back to life when added to water and it's really quite amazing to see! My favorites are peas... and celery! The carrots above were for Deb's Delectable Carrot Cake... check it out in our recipe section, it's delectable alright! Also check out Lori's Faster Pasta Prep coming up soon! Read how Lori rehydrated pasta - and how it can affect your budget's bottom line!

Re-hydrating Pasta

Although I don't do this myself, I did want to share this with you.

Re-hydrating pasta makes for "Fasta Pasta Prep!" (sorry, couldn't resist that) and a possible energy/water savings... according to Lori!

An interesting question regarding *re-hydrating* pasta for "faster pasta prep" came from Lori of Illinois: "Although I've been looking around I have not had any luck finding any reference to dehydrating cooked pasta. By that I mean in certain emergency situations, wouldn't food prep be faster and use less water if pasta (noodles, spaghetti, etc.) were also cooked, then dehydrated and packaged for long term storage? 'Instant' rice comes to mind as an example of a product already on store shelves (albeit they're in short term packaging). Any prohibitions to adding pasta products? Any special considerations in preparing/packaging/storing?"

This was my reply after I'd promised Lori I would cook some pasta, let it sit after vacuum-packing, and then re-hydrate/cook it again: "Today I cooked my 'previously-cooked-and-dehydrated al-dente pasta' and it took just about the same amount of cooking time in boiling water... so unfortunately, I can't see any benefit to dehydrating cooked pasta to save energy resources, sadly!"

But That Didn't Put Lori Off!!

Lori was supposed to be going out of town for a few weeks but wrote back with this: "I never made my trip out of town, an ear infection got in the way so while stranded at home I did dehydrate three different pastas, elbow macaroni, wide noodles, and the small mostaccioli.

"My dehydrator dried each of the three types in about 3 hours. I experimented with two temperature settings, one at 150 degrees (suggested by a backpacker) and the others at 135 degrees. Both turned out about the same, needing about 3 hours. The wide noodles were a thicker specialty brand, not the thin flat noodles, which I did at the higher temperature." Lori is using Nesco's newest Gardenmaster FD-1018P, a 1000-watt dehydrator which has a faster drying time. It will handle up to 30 trays. People who may try this at home using other makes and models may find their drying times are longer.

Experimentation Time...

Lori continues: "Let me have some time tomorrow to experiment. I did continue to search online after my initial contact with you and then discovered the backpack/hiking web sites where the food discussion threads were very helpful.

"The re-hydrating may take about the same amount of time, but as I recall, the backpacking board discussions pro vs con did point out that to rehydrate the pasta, less water was needed as opposed to when the pasta was originally cooked. When cooking, if too little water is used, then you see problems with the water getting starchy and the noodles sticking together.

"Maybe the real benefit and savings is with water usage and not fuel consumption. In a particular scenario - like people hiking or camping and to all those people out east after the hurricane and now have no electricity and their drinking water may be questionable and difficult to acquire - potable water resources could be an issue.

"I'm guessing that the investment in dehydrating cooked pasta will have value for the weekend warrior or casualties of mother-nature -- people whose need is outside the box of the typical money-saving homemaker."

Well, the final results are in

Lori says: "I just finished my first reconstitution test!"

Macaroni

"I put 1 cup of dehydrated macaroni into a small stainless steel bowl, then poured 1 cup of boiling water over the pasta, and covered the top of the bowl with a small plate to keep the heat and steam enclosed. Maybe next time I'll add a towel around the whole deal for added heat retention.

"I set a kitchen timer for 20 minutes, figuring it might take a tad longer to rehydrate since the water was no longer boiling. I removed the top 3-4 times to give the pasta a stir and make sure the macaroni had sufficient water available for maximum absorption. Maybe that was unnecessary after the initial 'pour, stir, and cover', it's just what I did out of curiosity because it was the first time I attempted this.

"After 10 minutes the pasta had that 'cooked look' and at 7 minutes left I had to taste test and would say the macaroni was at the 'al-dente' stage. I let the remaining time run out. The stainless steel bowl, of course, had cooled down some, but was easy to handle. The pasta was softer and more like what everyone is used to. I poured out the remaining water and ended up with 1/3 cup of slightly cloudy water.

"So to me it was a success"

"I only needed to boil 1 cup of water for my 1 cup of small macaroni pasta, with a small amount of water left over. Less energy consumption, a fraction of the water to finish it off, and then a 20 minute or so wait. So the hiker/backpacker has something going there and people stuck in a disaster situation can put food on the table faster and not squander their fresh drinking water which mostly gets thrown away if cooking using conventional methods.

"Additionally, the hikers also will use the zipper style freezer bags to reconstitute their dehydrated meals. No pots and pans! After adding water they can put their baggie into something called a 'Cozy' (typically a quilted cloth pocket) which insulates the cooking food until ready to eat."

Wide Noodles and Mostaccioli

"I measured out 1 cup each of the pasta. The noodles I snapped in half so to better get a full cup of pasta. I found smaller stainless bowls of the same size and put each on a pot holder, found some thicker terry kitchen dish towels to wrap (insulate) after the water was added. "I added 1 cup boiling water to each bowl, gave a good stir and covered the bowl top with a hard plastic cutting board. A towel was wrapped around the two adjacent bowls and two more were placed on top of the cutting board... so it was pretty hard for the heat to escape!

"Twenty and more minutes later (I got wrapped up in an episode of "Picker Sisters" on Lifetime ...oops!) I checked on the bowls. They were pretty much done and did need a little more stirring to separate some 'stick-togethers'. "Again, when draining off the excess there was about 1/3 cup of water from each bowl. The noodles are perfect and ready for use. Think 'cool kitchen' in August, little or no added humidity from pots of boiling water, and the AC not running more because of the added heat! So there is an energy savings of sorts.

"Hope my slightly different process of reconstituting and preparing will have some value to some of your readers."

Thank You, Lori, for sharing your faster pasta prep with us!

56
FREQUENTLY
ASKED
QUESTIONS

Q: What are the sheets for that go on the dehydrator trays?

A: There are two kinds of dehydrator sheets:

1) Solid plastic dehydrator sheets (to keep liquids from dripping down to lower trays). They are for runny foods such as apple sauce or our fruit roll mixes. The mesh is too open for this.

2) Criss-cross plastic dehydrator sheets (needed for ventilation) to keep sticky foods from sticking to the tray itself, for easier clean-up - also to keep smaller foods (like celery when it dries) from falling through to lower trays.

Q: What size oxygen packs to use for dehydrated food?

A: The reason for different sizes depends upon what size container your dehydrated foods are placed in. They are readily available in different sizes: 100cc, 300cc, and up.

Q: What happens to the oxygen absorbers when you open the bag?

A: When you open your Mylar bags to retrieve a package, if you do it quickly, and re-seal the Mylar bag straight away, you should be good to go until the next visit -- but if you'd rather be safe than sorry, then by all means, replace the old 300cc pack with a new one!

NOTE: When you use the 100cc oxy-packs in the mason jars, you can really hear the jar 'pop' when you open it - and that's how you know that the oxy-pack is still 'good'. Replace it when you don't hear the 'pop' any more.

Q: Are the oxygen packs sealed individually?

A: Yes. But they are shipped in quantities of 50, or 100. Some companies offer combo packs of 50 Mylar bags with 50 300-cc oxy-packs! Convenient!

Q: Are oxygen-packs safe, i.e. not poisonous?

A: They are totally safe!

Q: Can you store wheat?

A: You can store milled flour for five years - just follow our basic steps: vacuum bag it with an oxy-pack tucked in it, and then Mylar bag it, and then put away in buckets or bins.

Q: Can you vacuum noodles, rice, flour, and dry beans - and if so, how do I store them?

A: Yes to all! Even though the noodles, beans, etc. are dry to begin with, be advised to still use an oxy-pack as they do more than just remove oxygen, they help prevent mold and protect dry foods from insect damage. Store in air-tight mason jars, or in food-vacuum-sealer bags. I've even got salt and sugar 'stashed away'!

Q: I work during the day. Can I prepare veggies/fruit in the evening, store them in containers in the fridge overnight, then put them on the dehydrator before I leave for work in the morning?

A: Fantastic question, and the answer is YES! But remember, certain fruits and veggies need spraying with lemon juice, so do that before you put the lid on the container! See Dehydrating Fruit and Dehydrating Veggies for which ones need the juice.

Q: Can you re-use the ziplock bags after conditioning, as they're pretty expensive to use just the one time?

A: I have been reusing my bags for that very same reason - it's wrong to throw them away just after one use! However, having said that, I DO toss them if they have any sticky residue in them at all from previous fruits or veggies. I would NEVER re-use a bag that had meat in it previously.

Q: Can you Dehydrate Brussels Sprouts?

A: Yes! Even though I do not have Brussels Sprouts listed in this book, you can treat these 'miniature cabbages' (as I like to think of them!) like fresh Broccoli. Cut the Brussels Sprouts in half and follow the instructions on the Broccoli page.

Q: Can you Dehydrate Pumpkin?

A: Pumpkin can indeed be dehydrated, simply follow the same instructions we use for dehydrating butternut squash.

Q: Can I just put my dehydrated food in a zip-lock bag without an oxypack?

A: When we dehydrate food for long-term storage, it is highly recommended to include the oxypack in the vacuum-sealed bag. We then can leave this bag alone for weeks and months...

However, if you intend to eat the dehydrated foods within a few days or so, you can indeed just keep them in a plain old Ziploc bag without an oxygen pack. Fruit and veggies may not even need to be refrigerated, but dehydrated meat in an <u>un</u>vacuum-sealed zip lock bag will need to be refrigerated. Better to err on the safe side!

For foods I use on a regular basis such as my onions, celery, mixed veggies, that I keep in mason jars in my kitchen cupboards, I do use an oxypack in those mason jars. When I don't hear the 'pop' when I take off the lid, I know it's time to put in a new oxypack.

I do like to use the oxypacks in just about everything I'm vacuum sealing for the long-term, as they absorb any (stray) oxygen and keep the contents from spoiling (according to the manufacturers).

Q: Can you use pre made mixes for long term storage if I put it in individual jars with oxy absorbers? The spice mix that comes with pre packaged mixes like the boxed dinners or potatoes, should it be opened and poured in jar or left in its original package?

A: Any foods that are already packaged and have printed 'use-by' dates on them don't need vacuum sealing with an oxypack, and their expiration dates are what I'd follow. Certain pre-packaged food mixes may already have chemicals in them to act as preservatives, so I personally would not open up packets to save in jars.

Having said that, I have opened up bags of sugar, salt, and flour and have vacuum packed those with an oxy-pack thrown in... these items

I chose to vacuum pack to keep any rain water away, as I live in Florida and have been through a few (wet!) hurricanes!

This book is really trying to focus on fresh produce and how to dehydrate it and store it... and my aim personally is to start growing my own fruit and vegetables in the very near future.

There is nothing wrong with storing some boxed foods, just remember to keep rotating your stock!

Q: Although I've been looking around I have not had any luck finding any reference to dehydrating cooked pasta.
By that I mean in certain emergency situations wouldn't food prep be faster and use less water if pasta (noodles, spaghetti, etc.) were also cooked, then dehydrated and packaged for long term storage? Any prohibitions to adding pasta products? Any special considerations in preparing/packaging/storing?

A: Today I cooked my 'previously-cooked-and-dehydrated al-dente pasta' and it took just about the same amount of cooking time in boiling water... so unfortunately, I can't see any benefit to dehydrating cooked pasta to save energy resources, sadly!

(Read about Lori's way to save water usage when preparing pasta in the previous chapter).

Q: Do you know how to dehydrate grated Cheddar Cheese? If so can you put the directions online? Thank you so much.
A: Have a laugh at this: I had some grated cheese and decided to vacuum pack it (no dehydrating, just vacuumed it!) and the suction from the vacuum sealer squashed all the cheese together in one clump! Ugh! LOL! Yes you can dehydrate cheese, use the fruit-roll sheets to prevent it dropping through the tray.

You can buy dehydrated cheese (as in a powdered cheese sauce) at Honeyville Farms.

http://store.honeyvillegrain.com/powderedcheesecan.aspx#.UGcou 66oZ8E

For a shorter URL, just do a Google search for Honeyville Farms, and then browse for Powdered Cheese.

Q: When drying plums, what does "pop the back" mean?

A: Popping the back of the plums is simply this: When the plum is cut in half (and the pit removed), simply use your thumbs to turn the half "inside out" so the flesh is on the outside.

Q: Do you have any pointers on dehydrating green peas? My first batch of frozen peas don't want to re-hydrate; they have a small hard solid pit in the center. I dehydrated them at 130°F for about 10 hrs in an Excalibur with temp control and timer. They seemed a little rubbery at 8 hours so I added two more hours. Thanks for any input -- Steve

A: Steve and I came to the conclusion that he may need to cook the peas longer after re-hydrating - and Steve says he adds his peas to soups -- and his favorite: yellow rice! He adds the peas about ten minutes before the rice is done. And when Steve doesn't have much time for lunch at work, he makes a mix of dehydrated spinach, peas, celery, mushrooms and corn - puts it into a Ball® canning jar with an oxygen absorber in it - and adds it to ramen soups for lunch when he doesn't have time for anything else. "At least I will get some nutritional value from the dehydrated veggies" Steve says. "I add the veggies at the start and let it sit for 5 minutes after cooking." Great idea Steve! And thanks for writing in.

Q: If I store the dehydrated food exactly as you instructed... in plastic bins in my garage... how long will it last?

A: When dehydrated foods are vacuum-packed in quality bags with oxygen absorbers, Mylar bags, and airtight bins, you're good to go for years! The key is keeping light and moisture (and rodents!) away. Use opaque bins to help keep light out. Make sure to check your bags for any that may have punctured (a quick feel for any squishy bags is a giveaway, as all bags when vacuumed and sealed properly feel pretty hard) and remember to write the date on the food bags and rotate your stock!

Q: Can you dehydrate lettuce? If so can you tell me how? Will it rehydrate so you can use it for salad?

A: You can dehydrate cabbage, so I don't see why you couldn't dehydrate lettuce, in fact, anything that contains water can be dehydrated... but, having said "yes" to lettuce, I wouldn't recommend it. I will assume that upon re-hydrating the brittle lettuce leaves, they will turn to mush, rather like spinach when you wilt spinach leaves! Not much you can do with it (lettuce) aside from lettuce soup :-) If you have a go, please let us know how it turned out!

Q: My dehydrated foods - apples, potatoes, etc. pop the vacuum bag after it seals... not sure what to do?

A: It's annoying, to be sure, and can happen... and one thing to look out for is over-filling your vacuum bags. Also, try to make the contents lie as flat as you can, prior to filling. I do this by adding the dried food and its oxy pack to the bag, then clamping the bag in the vacuum sealer. Pat the top and bottom of the bag to make it (the contents) lie as flat as possible, before finally drawing the air out.

Also, check to see if your model of vacuum-sealer is maybe on too high a setting? Some models may have this feature, most do not, however.

Last comment is to check to make sure that you're not using 'cheap' bags!

Q: How long will vegetables keep when dehydrated and vacuum packed?

A: Dehydrated vegetables (and fruit) can last for weeks, and months, when packaged correctly.

First of all, use 3 Mil. 2-ply vacuum bags, (see chapter on Vacuum Sealer Bags for great bags), and don't forget to add the oxygen absorber... that is very important, as the absorbers keep the food safe by preventing mold-growth.

I find that rotating the food packages is the only way to go, so that means having a continual supply... using the oldest packages first, and putting subsequent foods clearly marked with a written date stamp on it. Magic markers are great for that!

Aim to have three months' supply, i.e. create a batch one month, label it. Create a second batch a month later, label it. Create the third batch the following month - label it, and so on - by this time you'll actually be using the first batch in your recipes etc.

Q: Can You Rehydrate Fruit at all?

A: Curtis wrote in to ask if you can rehydrate fruit. Yes you can, such as apples for apple pies. For the most part, we tend to eat dehydrated fruit as snacks, e.g. raisins, prunes, and apricots.

Q: Can You Dehydrate Eggs?

A: Yes Mariana, you can dehydrate eggs, and I believe you can do this safely at home by scrambling the eggs first (don't add anything to them), heat gently until cooked through, then dehydrate. Of course, an easier way is to simply buy dehydrated eggs! Here is a highly recommended site: Honeyville Farms

http://store.honeyvillegrain.com/powderedwholeeggscan.aspx#.UG coYa6oZ8E

For a shorter URL, just do a Google search for Honeyville Farms, and then browse for Powdered Eggs.

Q: HI! I'm new to dehydrating and have been having problems. I found your blog looking for answers! I've tried fruit leathers several different times, each one different. I keep getting holes in them. They come out looking like Swiss cheese! Have you had this? Any clue what I'm doing wrong? THANKS!

A: Hi Sara - sorry to hear you're getting holy leathers! You may have been dehydrating them on too low a setting - and remember they *do* take a long time to dehydrate due to the fact that it sits on a solid plastic sheet, so we've only got air on the top of the product instead of all around it. Hope this helps!

Q: I have an overheating dehydrator and looking for a work around. Also wondering if a full dehydrator is cooler than a partially filled one, or the temperature is cooler at the beginning because of moisture in the food? I have a problem with case hardening. Thanks.

A: First of all, you need to find out why the dehydrator IS overheating, is it faulty? Does it get extremely warm? If you suspect it's faulty - send it back for a replacement if it's still under warranty...

Second, the temperature IS set by the user and is kept constant by the sensor/thermostat, but, I agree with your suggestion that the air in the dehydrator would seem 'cooler' when you first start out due to the air in the dehydrator containing water and when the food dries out, the air could seem 'warmer'. A fully filled dehydrator will take longer to dry foods than a lesser filled one! :-)

And lastly, the case hardening is a sure sign of having the dehydrator on TOO high to begin with. It's very tempting to turn it up high to speed up the process! So turn it down to the recommended temperatures I give for each vegetable or fruit. THIS is where patience wins out! Thanks again for taking time to write in! :-)

Q: I'd like to dehydrate acorn squash. Do I cook and do it just like butternut squash? I can't find any info. for acorn squash... Thanks, Bret

A: Acorn squash is treated just like butternut squash, though it is a little harder to peel due to its shape... I slice the squash first into slices, then cut off the rind and remove the center seeds - and continue with the butternut squash instructions.

As with the watermelon seeds, you can also save the seeds of the squash (and pumpkin of course!)

Roast the seeds. Let them dry thoroughly after giving them a cleaning in your sieve under the kitchen faucet. Toss them on a cookie sheet for 15 to 20 minutes at 325°F. Spray the seeds first with plain cooking spray and a dash of salt. Best eaten when fully cooled.

This just back from Bret: "Susan, thanks for your help. I will be trying it this week! I plan on drying them and then run them through a blender to make it into a powder and then vacuum seal it. I think that will be great to add to dishes such as soups and stews for extra nutrition, especially if kids don't know what you added to their dinner! :-) Have a great day --Bret"

~*~

Since printing this book, there have been many more questions asked and their answers are posted on the site for your convenience.

NOTE: Please visit:
http://www.easy-food-dehydrating.com

or while at the site, go to the "What's New?" (blog) page:
http://www.easy-food-dehydrating.com/Food-Dehydrating-blog.html

and subscribe via RSS too!

Thank you.

57
EASY DEHYDRATED
FOOD RECIPES

We have many easy dehydrated food recipes that are tantalizing, mouth-watering and so e-a-s-y to make -- and we'd love to share a few of ours with you!

Check out these below -- choose an Easy Recipe -- and get cookin'!

Main Meals

BEEF STEW

BLACK BEAN SOUP

CARROT SOUP

CAULIFLOWER MASH

CAULIFLOWER SOUP

CELERY AND POTATO SOUP

CHICKEN NOODLE SOUP

CHICKEN SALAD

CURRIED CELERY AND POTATO SOUP

GREEN SPLIT PEA SOUP

LEMONY CHICKEN ORZO SOUP

LENTIL SOUP

POTATO AND BACON HASH

RATATOUILLE

SHEPHERD'S PIE

TASTY TUNA FISH SOUP

TUNA PASTA BAKE

TUNA SALAD

VEGETABLE SOUP

VELVETY PEA SOUP

Desserts

APPLE SAUCE

DEBBY'S DELECTABLE CARROT CAKE

MOM'S CRANBERRY AND PINEAPPLE PIE

Extras

ANITA'S SUPER EASY BREAD

HERBED BREAD

HOME-BAKED BREAD BEGINNER'S RECIPE

MILLET AND QUINOA

We hope you enjoy our easy-to-make recipes, and share them with your friends. Help us here at Easy-Food-Dehydrating to get the word out, that fruit and vegetables are so good for us, and we can dehydrate them when they're in season, or use the super standby of frozen vegetables for dehydrating too, when they're not as readily available!

I have been having a blast making my own bread too -- it's so satisfying to cut off a slice from one of your own loaves -- I keep mine in a clear plastic bread-saver on my kitchen counter, in part to save using plastic bags and ties, *but really because I like showing off the bread! :-)*

Beef Stew
in your slow-cooker

Ingredients for Beef Stew:

- 1/2 cup dehydrated carrots

- 1/2 cup dehydrated sliced potatoes

- 1/4 cup dehydrated onion

- 3 tablespoons dehydrated celery

- 2 slices dehydrated elephant garlic, crumbled

- 3/4 to 1 lb fresh stewing beef

- 3 cups beef stock (I choose to use Better Than Bouillon by Superior Touch)

- 2 tablespoons plain flour, mixed with 1/4 cup cold water

- seasonings: Italian (dried) herbs to taste (about 1/2 teaspoon)

- 1 tablespoon Worcestershire Sauce

- 1 tablespoon tomato paste (optional)

- 2 tablespoons tomato ketchup

- pepper (and salt*) to taste

Here's How To Make It!

Put the dehydrated items and seasonings in your crock-pot.

1) Prepare 3 cups beef stock in a large jug. Add the Worcestershire Sauce, ketchup, and optional tomato paste. Stir to dissolve the ketchup.

2) In a separate jug, measure 1/4 cup of cold water, add the flour, stir well then add this to the beef stock and Worcestershire Sauce and ketchup mix. Stir well.

3) Add the stock mix to the slow cooker (let it cool a bit so you don't shock your crock(pot)!

4) Add the stewing beef. Stir gently to mix all. Cover with crock-pot lid.

5) Turn on the slow cooker... low heat, 4 - 6 hours.

*IF you need to add salt, do so, BUT be careful NOT to over-salt as the bouillon has salt in it...When you return home from work... it's ready to serve! **NOTE: If you will be unable to check it during the day, make 4 cups of stock so it can cook for 8 hours and not dry out in the crock-pot.**

This stew is sooooo good – especially on those chilly Autumn and Winter evenings… sit by the fireside with a bowl of this and all's well with the world…

Please note that the quality of your stewing beef will determine the outcome. Good beef = melt-in-your-mouth beef stew.

It's OK for there to be some marbling in the meat!

Black Bean Soup
garnish with a blob of sour cream!

Ingredients for Black Bean Soup:

- 2 cans black beans

- 1 cup vegetable stock (I choose to use Better Than Bouillon by Superior Touch)

- 1/4 cup dehydrated onions

- 1/4 cup dehydrated celery

- 3 slices dehydrated elephant garlic, crumbled

- 2 slices fried bacon, crumbled

- good squirt of lemon juice

- 1 teaspoon cumin

- 1 teaspoon Worcestershire Sauce

- 1 teaspoon tomato ketchup

- salt* and pepper to taste

Here's How To Make It!

1) Re-hydrate the onions, celery, garlic, and drain well.

2) Cook the bacon in a saucepan, take it out when cooked and let it cool so you can crumble it up later.

3) Add the re-hydrated items to the pan and the bacon grease, cook for about five minutes.

4) Add the cup of vegetable stock.

5) Add the two cans of beans, drain them first but no need to rinse them. Add the Worcestershire Sauce and the ketchup, add the crumbled bacon.

6) Stir together well, simmer ten minutes, then add the lemon juice, salt and pepper to taste, and stir again... and serve with a blob of sour cream! Yummy!

*IF you need to add salt, do so, BUT be careful NOT to over-salt. The lemon juice adds that little zip of flavor...

Carrot Soup
with a dash of orange

Carrot Soup Ingredients:

- 2 tablespoons of olive oil

- 1-3/4 to 2 cups of dehydrated carrots

- 1/4 cup dehydrated onion

- 2 slices dehydrated elephant garlic, crumbled

- 1 teaspoon dried oregano

- 3-1/2 cups of vegetable stock. (I choose to use Better Than Bouillon by Superior Touch)

- salt and pepper to taste

- around 1/2 cup of fresh or from-concentrate orange juice, to taste. You should be able to 'detect' the orange juice, but not be overwhelmed by it.

Here's How To Make It!

1) Re-hydrate the dehydrated carrots, dehydrated onion, and the dehydrated garlic with clean cold or freshly boiled water.

2) To a good heavy pan, add the olive oil, medium heat.

3) Add the onions and carrots and cook until softened, around 8 minutes or so, then add the garlic and the oregano, and cook some more for a few minutes.

4) Add the vegetable stock and bring to a boil.

5) Simmer for 10 minutes or until the carrots and onion are cooked through.

6) Add the orange juice, stir.

7) Blend in a blender (I use my Cuisinart Blender) in small batches... allow air to escape from the little hole in the lid so that the heat doesn't cause any explosive problems! Just have your hand over that top little hole to catch any runaway splashes. Please understand, I am NOT saying "don't use the big lid", I'm saying don't use the "little clear plastic removable lid" which you use to add ingredients while the blender is running. I don't want this soup all over your kitchen! Just let the excess heat escape...

8) Blend until smooth, about 45 - 60 seconds.

Cauliflower Mash
just like mashed potatoes!

Ingredients for Cauliflower Mash:

- 2 cups dehydrated cauliflower

- 1/4 cup dehydrated onion

- 2 slices dehydrated elephant garlic

- 2 cups boiling water (for dehydrated items)

- 1/4 cup millet - rinse first

- 1/4 cup quinoa - rinse first

- pepper (and salt*) to taste

- 6 cups of vegetable stock (I choose to use Better Than Bouillon by Superior Touch)

Here's How To Make It!

1) Use the freshly boiled water to re-hydrate the dehydrated items above, in a glass bowl or measuring jug.

2) Rinse the millet and quinoa in a fine sieve, in the sink. Cook the millet and quinoa in about two cups of water in a heavy saucepan for about 20 minutes, stirring often, while the veggies re-hydrate. Add water if it dries up too fast!

3) Place the re-hydrated veggies in another saucepan, and add the vegetable stock and bring to a boil, then simmer for about 15-20 minutes, stirring often. NOTE: we're making 'mash' here, not a soup, so drain off excess water/stock -- save it for future use in a soup base! Remember to store the stock in your fridge, or freeze it in an ice-cube tray - that way you can add a cube of stock to a soup recipe!

4) Combine the millet/quinoa mix with the cauliflower mix - and mash to your desired smoothness!

If you're using a non-stick saucepan as I do, please mash this in a pan that isn't non-stick, or use a glass bowl -- prevent scratches in your non-stick (expensive) pans at all costs!

*IF you need to add salt, do so, BUT be careful NOT to over-salt as the bouillon has salt in it...

Cauliflower Soup
smooth and rich!

Cauliflower Soup Ingredients:

- 2 cups dehydrated cauliflower

- 1/8 cup dehydrated onion

- 1/8 cup dehydrated celery

- 2 slices dehydrated elephant garlic

- 2 cups boiling water (for the dehydrated items)

- 1/8 cup millet, optional - rinse first

- 1/8 cup quinoa, optional - rinse first

- pepper (and salt*) to taste

- 4 cups of vegetable stock (I choose to use Better Than Bouillon by Superior Touch)

- seasonings: 1/2 teaspoon Cumin, 2 tablespoons fresh chopped parsley, and a sprig for garnish!

Here's How To Make It!

1) Use the freshly boiled water to re-hydrate the dehydrated items above.

2) When they are sufficiently plump, put the veggies into a heavy saucepan (with the optional millet and quinoa -- RINSE the millet and quinoa first in a fine-sieve in the sink to get rid of the bitter taste).

3) Add the chopped parsley, vegetable stock, and cumin, and cook for 15-20 minutes, until the cauliflower is fully cooked/soft.

4) Let it cool a bit and blend (I use my Cuisinart Blender) in small batches... allow air to escape from the little hole in the lid so that the heat doesn't cause any explosive problems! Just have your hand over that top little hole to catch any runaway splashes. Please understand, I am NOT saying "don't use the big lid", I'm saying don't use the "little clear plastic removable lid" which you use to add ingredients while the blender is running. I don't want this soup all over your kitchen! Just let the excess heat escape...

5) Blend until smooth, about 45 - 60 seconds. Serve with an added sprig of parsley for garnish! *IF you need to add

salt, do so, BUT be careful NOT to over-salt as the bouillon has salt in it...

Celery and Potato Soup
a pinch of Tarragon makes all the difference

Ingredients for Celery and Potato Soup:

- 2 cups dehydrated potatoes

- 1 cup dehydrated celery

- 1/4 cup dehydrated onion

- 2 cups boiling water to rehydrate items above

- pepper (and salt*) to taste

- 4 cups of vegetable stock (I choose to use Better Than Bouillon by Superior Touch)

- seasonings: 1/2 teaspoon Cumin, 2 tablespoons fresh chopped parsley (or 1 teaspoon dried), 1/4 teaspoon Tarragon, 1/4 teaspoon Celery Salt

Here's How To Make It!

1) Use the freshly boiled water to re-hydrate the dehydrated items above.

2) When they are sufficiently plump, put the veggies into a heavy saucepan, toss the excess water, and add the vegetable stock to the pan.

3) Add the chopped parsley, tarragon, celery salt, and cumin. Bring to a boil and simmer for about 30 minutes, or until the vegetables are fully cooked/soft.

4) Let it cool a bit and blend (I use my Cuisinart Blender) in small batches... allow air to escape from the little hole in the lid. Keep your hand over that top little hole to catch any runaway splashes. Please understand, I am NOT saying "don't use the big lid. I don't want this soup all over your kitchen! Just let the excess heat escape... Blend until smooth, about 45 - 60 seconds.*IF you need to add salt, do so, BUT be careful NOT to over-salt as the bouillon has salt in it...

Chicken Noodle Soup
A Hearty Bowlful of Goodness

Chicken Noodle Soup Ingredients:

- 1/4 cup dehydrated carrots

- 1/8 cup dehydrated onion

- 2 tablespoons dehydrated celery

- 1 slice dehydrated elephant garlic

- 3 cups chicken stock (I choose to use Better Than Bouillon by Superior Touch)

- 1-1/2 cups whole wheat or regular egg noodles

- 2 tablespoons olive oil

- 1/2 lb pre-cooked dehydrated chicken or left-over chicken from last night's dinner! At a pinch use canned chicken in water, and crumble it up -- works FINE!

- seasonings: Italian (dried) herbs to taste (about 1/2 teaspoon)

- pepper (and salt*) to taste

Here's How To Make It!

1) Use clean cold water or freshly boiled water to re-hydrate the dehydrated items above.

2) When they are sufficiently plump, add the olive oil to a heavy pan on medium heat.

3) Add the onion and celery, cook for about 5 minutes.

4) Add the chicken stock, then add the garlic - crumbled finely, and the carrots, egg noodles, Italian herbs - and lest we forget, the chicken! Then cook an additional 8 minutes.

*IF you need to add salt, do so, BUT be careful NOT to over-salt as the bouillon contains salt. There's something about chicken soup -- doesn't matter what time of the year you have it -- it soothes the soul, mends a cold, and fixes a broken heart! Serve with your own fresh baked bread!

Chicken Salad
go grab that freshly-baked bun!

Ingredients for our tasty Chicken Salad:

- 1 tablespoon dehydrated celery

- 1/2 tablespoon dehydrated red onion

- 1/2 of a 12.5 oz can of canned chicken breast

- 2 tablespoons real Mayonnaise

- 3 tablespoons regular or reduced fat sour cream

- 3 tablespoons ricotta cheese

- 1/2 - 1 teaspoon prepared yellow mustard (optional)

- seasonings: salt and ground black pepper to taste

Here's How To Make It!

1) Use clean cold water re-hydrate the celery and red onion.

2) When plump, put in a medium sized glass bowl, add the mayonnaise, sour cream, ricotta cheese, and mustard - stir well.

3) Add the chicken, crumble it in a bit as you go, squeezing out any excess liquid. Stir ingredients to mix in the chicken.

4) Place in an airtight tub in the fridge to chill.

What makes this an easy recipe is the convenience of canned chicken. These cans of chicken last for years (check the date stamp always) and are a great stand-in for fresh chicken.

Think about adding dehydrated cranberries and sliced almonds to this! Serve it on our fantastic Fresh Bread coming up in the Extras section.

Either way, it's a winner of a sandwich and is ideal for picnics by the lake, or in your own backyard under the sun umbrella! If you happen to have a couple of spare cans of tuna lying around, then make our tasty tuna salad too! Whenever tuna and chicken cans go on sale, you can bet I stock up on them, and so should you -- put it away at today's prices, because you don't know how much more they will cost next week, or next month.

Curried Celery and Potato Soup
an alternative to our plain celery and potato soup

Curried Celery and Potato Soup Ingredients:

• 2 cups dehydrated potatoes

• 1 cup dehydrated celery

• 1/4 cup dehydrated onion

• 2 cups boiling water to rehydrate items above

• 2 oz orzo (optional)

• pepper (and salt*) to taste

• 4 cups of vegetable stock (I choose to use Better Than Bouillon by Superior Touch)

- seasonings: 1/2 teaspoon Cumin, 1/2 tablespoon curry powder (or more, to taste), 1/2 teaspoon Turmeric, 1/4 teaspoon Tarragon

Here's How To Make It!

1) Use the freshly boiled water to re-hydrate the dehydrated items above.

2) When they are sufficiently plump, put the veggies into a heavy saucepan, toss the excess water, and add the vegetable stock to the pan.

3) Add the curry, turmeric, tarragon, and cumin and the optional orzo. Bring to a boil and simmer for about 30 minutes, or until the vegetables are fully cooked/soft. At this point, we decided to eat it 'as is', rather than blend it, but you can blend it if you wish!

4) Let it cool a bit and blend (I use my Cuisinart Blender) in small batches ... allow air to escape from the little hole in the lid so that the heat doesn't cause any explosive problems! Just have your hand over that top little hole to catch any runaway splashes. Please note, I am NOT saying "don't use the big lid", I'm saying don't use the "little clear plastic removable lid" which you use to add ingredients while the blender is running. I don't want this soup all over your kitchen! Just let the excess heat escape...

5) Blend until smooth, about 45 - 60 seconds.

*IF you need to add salt, do so, BUT be careful NOT to over-salt as the bouillon has salt in it...

Green Split Pea Soup
great soup for the slow-cooker!

Ingredients for Green Split Pea Soup:

- 16 oz. bag of green split peas

- 1/4 cup dehydrated carrots

- 1/4 cup dehydrated onion

- 1/4 cup dehydrated celery

- 2 slices dehydrated elephant garlic

- 2 cups boiling water (for dehydrated items)

- pepper (and salt*) to taste

- a couple handfuls of chopped ham

- 6 cups of ham-base stock (I choose to use Better Than Bouillon by Superior Touch)

Here's How To Make It!

1) Use the freshly boiled water to re-hydrate the dehydrated items above.

2) When they are sufficiently plump, put the veggies and their water in your slow cooker/crock-pot.

3) Add the ham stock and let it cool down a bit so you don't shock your crock(pot)!

4) Add the green split peas (check for stones, other foreign objects first!) Stir with wooden spoon.

*IF you need to add salt, do so, BUT be careful NOT to over-salt as the bouillon contains salt.

Cook in the slow cooker/crock-pot on low heat all day - and you come home to the most delicious, smooth pea soup to be savored with a slice of bread 'n' butter!

Don't forget you can use yellow split peas too - for a change - and this recipe lends itself to lentils just as easily, though I do have a lentil soup recipe coming up for you to savor. I love making this soup - it tastes so good - and it is very easy on the pocketbook.

This will serve about 4 hungry people, or six, if you're having a sandwich along with it.

Leftovers?

It tends to thicken quite a bit overnight in the fridge, so add a little water to it if you wish to make it a little thinner.

Lemony Chicken Soup
with a dash of lemon!

Lemony Chicken Orzo Soup Ingredients:

- slice dehydrated elephant garlic

- 1 tablespoon dehydrated onion

- 1 tablespoon dehydrated carrots, crumbled into small pieces

- 3 cups chicken stock (I choose to use Better Than Bouillon by Superior Touch)

- 1 cup orzo

- 2 tablespoons olive oil

- 1/4 lb pre-cooked dehydrated chicken or leftover chicken from last night's dinner! You can use canned chicken in water too - works great!

- seasonings: Italian (dried) herbs to taste (about 1/4 teaspoon)

- handful fresh chopped parsley

- pepper (and salt*) to taste

- lemon juice, or dehydrated lemon, or lemon zest

Here's How To Make It!

1) Use clean cold water or freshly boiled water to re-hydrate the dehydrated items above.

2) When they are sufficiently plump, add the olive oil to a heavy pan on medium heat.

3) Add the onion and carrots, cook for about 5 minutes.

4) Add the chicken stock, then add the garlic - crumbled finely, and the remaining ingredients - Bring to a boil and cook an additional 8 minutes.

5) At the end of cooking, add a good squirt of lemon juice (I choose to use RealLemon brand). We just need to detect a taste of lemon in the soup, and not overwhelm it with lemon! If you prefer, you can use the zest of fresh lemons or use a dash of lemon from your dehydrated lemon stock!

*IF you need to add salt, do so, BUT be careful NOT to over-salt as the bouillon has salt in it.

And yes, sin of all sins, I WAS sitting in front of the computer eating it when I took the recipe photo... and NOT at the dining table! But no matter where you eat this soup, it's always refreshing and delicious, and it's that touch of lemon that elevates it from ordinary chicken soup, to extraordinary lemon chicken soup!

NOTE: If you're out of orzo, you can very easily substitute white rice for the orzo, though the rice will need about 5 to 10 minutes more to cook through. I just like the way the orzo plumps up so big!

Lentil Soup
made in your slow-cooker

Ingredients for Lentil Soup:

- 16 oz. bag of lentils

- 1/4 cup dehydrated carrots

- 1/4 cup dehydrated onion

- 1/4 cup dehydrated celery

- 2 slices dehydrated elephant garlic

- 2 cups boiling water (for dehydrated items)

- 2 tablespoons olive oil

- pepper (and salt*) to taste

- 6 cups of vegetable stock (I choose to use Better Than Bouillon by Superior Touch)

- seasonings: 1/2 teaspoon Marjoram, 1/4 teaspoon Oregano

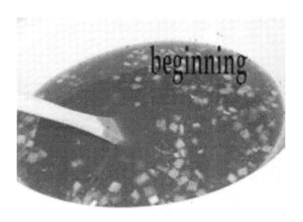

Here's How To Make It!

1) Use the freshly boiled water to re-hydrate the dehydrated items above.

2) When they are sufficiently plump, put the veggies and their water in your slow cooker/crock-pot.

3) Make the vegetable stock (while the items re-hydrate) and then let the stock cool down a bit so you don't shock your crock(pot)!

4) Add the lentils (check for stones, other foreign objects first! though I have yet to find 'foreign' objects but it's printed on the bag for a good reason!)

5) Add the seasonings and olive oil, stir with wooden spoon.

*IF you need to add salt, do so, BUT be careful NOT to over-salt as the bouillon has salt in it...

Cook in the slow cooker/crock-pot on low heat all day -- about 7 hrs -- and you come home to a delicious ready-cooked meal!

As an alternative to the brown lentils, try splurging on the orange lentils! It tastes just a little bit different, and is a warmer shade than brown.

I love making these easy lentil soups because not only do they taste great, they are very filling, and they are easy on the wallet.

This huge batch of soup should feed six people, with a half-sandwich on the side.

Potato and Bacon Hash
the perfect Sunday Brunch

Potato and Bacon Hash Ingredients:

- 1-1/2 cups dehydrated sliced potatoes

- 1/4 cup dehydrated onion

- 2 slices dehydrated elephant garlic

- 4 slices bacon (or 2 oz. corned beef, or ham)

- 1 tablespoon plain flour

- 2 tablespoons tomato ketchup

- 1 tablespoon Worcestershire Sauce

- 4 oz. grated cheddar cheese

- 1/4 cup cold water

231

• salt and pepper to taste

Here's How To Make It!

1) In a large saucepan, add the dehydrated sliced potatoes, onion, and elephant garlic. Add boiling water to cover them all. Let them re-hydrate in the pan, add more boiling water if necessary.

2) Fry up the bacon!

3) While the bacon is cooking, combine the flour and water in a measuring jug, add the ketchup and Worcestershire sauce and set aside.

4) When the potato mix is sufficiently re-hydrated (and remember, the potatoes are already cooked prior to dehydrating so they only need to be heated through), add the ketchup mix and gently stir and cook a few minutes more.

5) Add the bacon, crumbled (or any other flavorful meat!)

6) Season with salt and pepper to taste.

7) Sprinkle on about 4 oz grated cheddar cheese, let it melt and serve!

...and I'll be right over to your house for some!

This is a fun meal to make on a leisurely Sunday morning; it drives people mad with the sizzling bacon aroma, and by the time it's ready, it is devoured with lightning speed!

It's a pretty hearty meal, and it makes a great brunch -- take it outside and enjoy the fresh air! The potato and bacon hash dish will fill you up, and keep you going easily until the dinner time evening meal.

You can substitute the bacon for canned corned beef, but watch the corned beef from sticking to the bottom of the pan.

Ratatouille
for the Mediterranean in your kitchen

Ingredients for Ratatouille:

- 1-1/2 cups dehydrated zucchini

- 1whole fresh eggplant, cubed (I leave the skin on, so wash well first)

- 1/2 cup dehydrated onion rings

- 1/4 cup dehydrated mushrooms

- 10 black olives, cut in half

- 3 slices dehydrated elephant garlic, crumbled

- boiling water (for dehydrated items)

- 2 tablespoons olive oil

- pepper (and salt*) to taste

- 1 14.5 oz. can small-diced tomatoes

- 1 cup of vegetable stock (I choose to use Better Than Bouillon by Superior Touch)

- seasonings: 1 tablespoon dried Italian Herb blend (more or less, to taste)

- NOTE: Optional Orzo, 1 cup

Here's How To Make It!

1) Use the freshly boiled water to re-hydrate the dehydrated items above, let sit until they have plumped up.

2) Put oil in a large saucepan, sauté the eggplant.

3) Pour off excess water from dehydrated veggies, and add the veggies carefully to your saucepan as water can spit in hot oil...

4) Add 1 cup of vegetable stock, and add the Italian seasoning.

5) Add the sliced olives and the mushrooms.

6) Cook for 15 minutes or until the vegetables are tender.

If adding the orzo, add this at step 4. You may need to add a little more boiled water too, if you find the orzo drinks up your stock too soon. Orzo only needs around 10 minutes to cook, half the time of rice. This makes this Ratatouille dish like a risotto, to me!
*IF you need to add salt, do so, BUT be careful NOT to over-salt as the bouillon has salt in it...

As an alternative to the orzo, make some white or brown rice to serve with these vegetables. This dish smells so good when it is cooking; it fills your kitchen with a very pleasant aroma of the Mediterranean!

You can eat this just as a vegetable side dish, but with the addition of the rice or orzo, it makes a whole meal. Our family loves this!

Shepherd's Pie
in individual ramekins

Shepherd's Pie Ingredients:

- 1 lb lean ground beef

- 2 tablespoons olive oil

- 1/2 cup dehydrated onion

- 1/2 cup dehydrated celery

- 1 cup dehydrated carrots

- 2 cups boiling water (for the dehydrated items)

- 2 tablespoons plain flour

- 2 tablespoons Worcestershire Sauce

- 2 tablespoons tomato ketchup

- 1 tablespoon tomato paste

- pepper (and salt*) to taste

- 1-1/2 cups of beef stock (I choose to use Better Than Bouillon by Superior Touch)

- 5 medium white potatoes, peeled, quartered

- knob of butter

- dash whole milk

- salt and pepper to taste

Here's How To Make It!

1) Use the freshly boiled water to re-hydrate the dehydrated items above, then discard this water.

2) When they are sufficiently plump, put the veggies into a heavy saucepan with the heated olive oil, and cook for five minutes.

3) Add the ground beef, and cook until the meat is browned through.

4) Make the beef stock, add the ketchup, tomato paste, and Worcestershire Sauce; add this to the saucepan and cook for 10 minutes.

5) In a small jug, add the flour and enough cold water to have a runny mixture (1/4 cup approx. of water).

6) In a separate pan, add the peeled and quartered potatoes, add pinch of salt, and bring to a boil and simmer until cooked through. Discard the water, add salt and pepper to taste, along with the pat of butter, and a dash of milk. We're just making regular mashed potatoes here!

7) When the beef in step 4 has cooked through, add the flour/water mix and stir thoroughly - the beef mixture will now thicken up nicely -- cook for a few minutes to make sure you don't have raw flour! Add salt/pepper to taste.

8) Spoon out the beef mixture into four ramekins and top with the mashed potatoes. Place ramekins under the broiler (not too close!) and broil until the peaks of the mashed potatoes turn brown... Enjoy!

*IF you need to add salt, do so, BUT be careful NOT to over-salt as the bouillon has salt in it...

Tuna Fish Soup
so easy to make!

Ingredients for Tasty Tuna Fish Soup:

- 1/4 cup dehydrated onion

- 1/4 cup dehydrated celery

- 1/2 cup dehydrated diced hash brown potatoes

- 2 slices dehydrated elephant garlic, crumbled

- 2 5-oz. cans tuna (I used one in oil and one in water)

- 4 cups clam or fish stock (I choose to use Better Than Bouillon by Superior Touch)

- 2 14.5 oz. cans small-diced tomatoes

- seasonings: 1/2 teaspoon dried Thyme

- 1/4 teaspoon white pepper (optional)

- (and salt*) to taste

Here's How To Make It!

1) Re-hydrate the onions, celery, garlic, and potatoes in 2 cups of clam stock (taste-test this stock, you don't need as much of it as you do of the other stocks I use) - for about 30 minutes.

2) Put in a tall saucepan, add remaining stock.

3) Bring to a boil, simmer 10 minutes.

4) Add the two cans of tuna. As noted in the ingredients above, I used one can of tuna in oil. I let half of the oil go into the soup from the tuna-in-oil can and all of the water in the tuna-in-water can.

5) Add the two cans of diced tomatoes and Thyme and White Pepper.

6) Simmer 5 more minutes, or until veggies are tender.

*IF you need to add salt, do so, BUT be careful NOT to over-salt as the clam bouillon is quite salty-tasting... This is a super-quick soup to make for lunch! I've always enjoyed clam chowders and New England (white!) chowders, but they are a bit more complicated to make than this... and out of a time-crunch necessity came this recipe! Plus it's a great way to use up dehydrated hash-brown (diced) potatoes. I hope you'll agree that it lives up to its title of 'tasty' tuna fish soup!

See next page for Tuna Fish Soup
with Smoked Paprika!

Tuna Fish Soup with Smoked Paprika

A variation of the super tasty tuna fish soup!

Use the same ingredients for the Tasty Tuna Fish Soup recipe, with the addition of 1 tablespoon of smoked paprika but omit the two cans of diced tomatoes.

Also, I used all the oil in the tuna-in-oil can -- I decided not to discard half of it as stated in the recipe -- bearing in mind that fish oil is very good for us!

OK, so the oil isn't exactly FROM the fish, but it's been hanging around the fish in the can!

Tuna Pasta Bake
from John in Derbyshire, UK

Ingredients for Tuna Pasta Bake:

- 2 cans tuna in water

- 1/4 cup dehydrated onion

- 3 large slices dehydrated elephant garlic

- 1 14.5 oz. can small-diced tomatoes

- handful dehydrated mushrooms

- 4 oz. whole wheat rotini (that spirally pasta!)

- 2 teaspoons of vegetable stock (I choose to use Better Than Bouillon by Superior Touch) to flavor the pasta cooking water

- tablespoon red wine (optional)

- seasoning: Italian dried herbs - a good pinch or two to taste

- olive oil as needed

- 4 oz. crème fraiche, OR plain yogurt, OR sour cream

- dash of black pepper

for the topping:
- 4 oz. approx. coarse shredded sharp cheddar cheese

- 2 slices bread, made into bread crumbs

Here's How To Make It!

1) Re-hydrate the onion, garlic, and mushrooms in a jug of cold water.

2) Drain the tuna as best you can in the kitchen sink, use a sieve.

3) Cook the pasta in the vegetable stock for TEN minutes, no more! Drain, place in oven-safe dish.

4) While the pasta is cooking, in a saucepan with about a tablespoon or two of olive oil, fry your breadcrumbs until golden and crisp. Takes a couple of minutes. Remove from pan and put aside in a small dish.

5) In the now-empty saucepan, add about 2 tablespoons olive oil, sauté the onion, garlic and mushrooms, until soft. Add the can of tomatoes, and Italian herbs, to taste. Add black pepper, to taste. Simmer for ten minutes.

6) Add the two cans of tuna to the pasta, and combine - breaking up the bigger tuna pieces. Add the sauce. Next,

add the crème fraiche (or sour cream, or plain yogurt), stir gently!

7) Smooth out the pasta and sauce, and add the grated cheese as a layer.

8) Add the breadcrumbs on top of the cheese.

9) Bake, uncovered, at 350°F for 30 minutes.

This fantastic tummy-pleasin' dish came to us from John, in Derbyshire, UK! He says "there's nothing like the sound of the breadcrumbs' crunch as your spoon dips down into the creamy pasta". And we couldn't agree more.

Tuna Salad
on freshly-baked sliced bread

Ingredients for Tuna Salad:

- 2 cans tuna in water

- 1 tablespoon dehydrated celery

- 1 tablespoon dehydrated red or white onion

- 3 tablespoons sour cream

- 2 tablespoons mayonnaise

- dash of salt and pepper

Here's How To Make It!

1) Re-hydrate the celery and onion in a jug of cold water.

2) Drain the tuna as best you can in the kitchen sink, use a sieve or squeeze out excess water with your hands.

3) Spoon out the mayo and sour cream in a dish and mix well with the celery and onion.

4) Add the two cans of tuna, and blend in!

5) Season with salt and pepper, and chill in the fridge.

I find that adding the onion and the celery give the salad a nice crunch! Spread some of this tuna fish salad on some of your very own homemade bread! Yes, you can easily make your own bread, and we've been doing it for a while now... there's such a sense of fulfillment in knowing that what you're eating has been 'prepared from scratch' and not out of cardboard boxes.

Check out the 'beginner' bread recipe at:

http://www.breadworld.com/Recipe.aspx?id=235

which we have used a few times and it tastes awesome... and Anita's Super Easy Bread (coming up soon in the "extras" section, page 261) which is what I make all the time now!

Just mix it up in a bowl, leave it alone for 2 hrs, then bake it for 25 minutes. It doesn't get much easier than that! The hard part is actually waiting for the bread to cool down... :-)

Vegetable Soup
(with added chicken)

Vegetable Soup Ingredients:

- 1/2 cup dehydrated carrots

- 1/2 cup dehydrated green beans

- 1/4 cup dehydrated onion

- 2 tablespoons dehydrated celery

- 2 slices dehydrated elephant garlic

- 1/2 cup dehydrated diced hash brown potatoes

- 1/2 cup cabbage (optional)

- 1 can of great northern beans, or whatever you like such as kidney beans etc.

- 4 cups vegetable stock (I choose to use Better Than Bouillon by Superior Touch)

- 1 cup whole wheat or regular egg noodles

- 2 tablespoons olive oil

- seasonings: Italian (dried) herbs to taste (about 1/2 teaspoon)

- pepper (and salt*) to taste

Here's How To Make It!

1) Use clean cold water or freshly boiled water to re-hydrate the dehydrated items above.

2) When they are sufficiently plump, add the olive oil to a heavy pan on medium heat.

3) Add the onion and celery, cook for about 5 minutes.

4) Add the vegetable stock, then add the garlic - crumbled finely, and the carrots, potato, egg noodles, Italian herbs - then cook an additional 8 minutes.

5) Add the can of beans of your choice towards the end of the cooking time in step 4, just to warm them through. Rinse your beans first! This helps in the 'gas' department...

*IF you need to add salt, do so, BUT be careful NOT to over-salt as the bouillon has salt in it...

It's ready to eat! Nothing beats a hot bowl of nutritious vegetable soup, whether from fresh vegetables, frozen vegetables, OR dehydrated vegetables!

The photo I used under the recipe title
shows some cooked chicken
I added at the last minute,
you could add ham, or turkey...
or just leave it as is!

Velvety Pea Soup
(one of my dad's favorites)

Ingredients for Velvety Pea Soup:

- 1 tablespoon of olive oil

- 1/4 cup dehydrated onion

- 3/4 teaspoon dried tarragon

- 1 cup of dehydrated peas

- 3 cups of vegetable stock (I choose to use Better Than Bouillon by Superior Touch)

- pepper (and salt*) to taste

Here's How To Make It!

1) Use clean cold water or freshly boiled water to re-hydrate the onion and peas, in separate bowls.

2) When they are sufficiently plump, add the olive oil to a heavy pan on medium heat.

3) Add the onions and cook until softened, around 5 minutes or so.

4) Add the vegetable stock and tarragon, bring to a boil.

5) Add the peas and simmer for 10 minutes or until the peas and onion are cooked through.

6) Blend in a blender (I use my Cuisinart Blender) in small batches... allow air to escape from the little hole in the lid so that the heat doesn't cause any explosive problems! Just have your hand over that top little hole to catch any runaway splashes. Please understand, I am NOT saying "don't use the big lid", I'm saying don't use the "little clear plastic removable lid" which you use to add ingredients while the blender is running. I don't want this soup all over your kitchen! Just let the excess heat escape...

7) Blend until smooth, about 45 - 60 seconds.

*IF you need to add salt, do so, BUT be careful NOT to over-salt as the bouillon has salt in it...

ENJOY! ... so quick and easy to prepare!
It's that little bit of tarragon, I think, that makes it special and credit for that idea goes to Ellie Krieger - she has some fantastic recipe books, you should really check them out.

59
DESSERTS

Apple Sauce
a dessert – or a sauce for roast pork

Apple Sauce Ingredients:

- 1 apple, peeled and diced

- dash of cinnamon

- 1.5 teaspoons of lemon juice

- tablespoon of water

- handful of dehydrated cranberries

- handful of raisins

- 2 dessertspoons brown sugar

- 1 tablespoon apricot jam

Here's How To Make It!

1) Peel the apple, dice into small to medium pieces.

2) Put in a non-stick pan and add the lemon juice, toss.

3) Add the water and cinnamon, stir well.

4) Add the raisins and cranberries, stir and cook about five minutes.

5) Add the brown sugar, stir, heat on low a minute.

6) Add the apricot jam, stir well and serve!

This sauce is so easy to make!

We enjoyed this apple sauce straight from the pan, spooned right over some French vanilla ice cream –

H E A V E N !

Double up the recipe ingredient amounts, as the quantity above was good for two people...

And yes, you can omit the apricot jam, but honestly, it adds a little zing, and thickens the juice. Try marmalade for a change!

And don't forget, this apple sauce works well as a sauce/dressing on roast pork too!

Debby's Delicious Carrot Cake
sinful...

Ingredients for Debby's Delectable Carrot Cake:

• 2 cups sugar

• 1/2 cups cooking oil

• 4 eggs

• 1 teaspoon cinnamon

• 2 teaspoons baking soda

• 1 teaspoon salt

• 2 cups plain flour

• 3 cups re-hydrated well-drained finely grated carrots (about 1-1/2 cups of dehydrated finely-grated carrots)

- 1 cup chopped walnuts

For The Frosting:

- 2 8-oz blocks of cream cheese

- 2 16-oz. boxes 10x confectioner's sugar

- 1 teaspoon vanilla

Here's How To Make It!

NOTE: First, set out the cream cheese to let it come to room temperature, chop the nuts, and rehydrate the carrots.

1) Mix well the first three ingredients: sugar, oil, and eggs.

2) Add in the next four ingredients: cinnamon, baking soda, salt, flour.

3) Stir in by hand the next two ingredients: carrots and walnuts.

4) Bake at 350°F for 45 minutes, in a 9"x 12" baking dish/pan.

5) Mix the frosting ingredients together: cream cheese, confectioner's sugar, vanilla.

6) Frost the cake with half the frosting while it is still warm (let it seep into the cake!) - Frost with remaining frosting when cake has cooled completely - and refrigerate.

And let's see how long this cake hangs around your home!

NOTE: *Credit for this recipe goes to Debby Wilson who kindly shared this fantastic carrot cake recipe with us!*

Cranberry and Pineapple Pie
great holiday dessert pie

Cranberry and Pineapple Pie Ingredients:

- 1 cup whole cranberry sauce (or 1/2 cup dehydrated cranberries, re-hydrated)

- 1 eight-oz. can crushed unsweetened pineapple, drained

- 1 three-oz. pkg raspberry-flavor gelatin

- 1 cup boiling water

- 1 9" graham cracker crust

- 2 cups miniature marshmallows

- 1/4 cup sweetened condensed milk

- 1/2 teaspoon vanilla extract

- 1 cup of whipped heavy-whipping cream

Here's How To Make It!

1) Get a glass bowl and dissolve the raspberry gelatin in a cup of boiling water. Stir in the cranberry sauce. (Rehydrate the cranberries first until they are plump if you're using your dehydrated cranberries) and then add the drained pineapple.

2) Put this in the fridge to set.

3) In a heavy pan, combine the condensed milk, mini marshmallows and stir over a low to medium heat until the marshmallows have melted.

4) Take off the heat and add the vanilla.

5) Put into a large bowl and cover it and let it stand until cooled to room temperature.

6) Whisk in a third of the whipped cream until smooth. Keep at it until it's smooth! Then fold in the remaining cream and spread over the cranberry-pineapple-raspberry gelatin mix in the pie crust.

7) Refrigerate the pie until it's set...

and ENJOY! ... it takes time but it's soooooo worth the wait! Mom wants you to know that credit for this recipe goes to Eddie Stott of Mt. Juliet, Tennessee -- Thanks! This is my favorite holiday dessert pie, though we don't save it just for holidays anymore! :-)

mom always makes this pie at Christmas time!

I love the sweetness of the pineapple and the condensed milk, followed by the tartness of the cranberries! Simply delicious... Add the creaminess of the topping -- the marshmallow, milk, and cream -- heavenly!

Home Baked Bread
*there's nothing like the aroma of
freshly-baked bread...*

Let's learn how to bake your own bread and save money just like my friend over in the UK! He loves to cook and bake. He sent me some great photos of his latest batch of bread and it just made my mouth water looking at it!

I decided it was high time to try my hand (again) at bread making. I did have a go when I was a kid, and they turned out like loaves of bricks. That put me off for 30 years!

Survive and Save Money - Bake your own Bread

But by making my own bread I can certainly save money and not have to rely on the grocery stores' high-priced breads. Mom and I figured it cost me around $1 per loaf, and about ten cents each per bun! WOW!

My husband researched for me and came across this fantastic bread recipe over at Bread World:

http://www.breadworld.com/Recipe.aspx?id=235

Easy To Do!

It is quite easy to bake your own bread, by the way. I could have made it much easier on myself if I had not been doing two loads of laundry and making up my husband's lunch bag at the same time! My mom and I could not wait for the bread to cool down completely. Excitedly we grabbed the bread knife and cut the first slice... or two, or three...

Beautiful Bread!

We were BOTH extremely impressed with the bread recipe and my efforts! It looked like real bakers had baked it! :-) By the way, I split the bread dough into three parts, two equal sized dough balls for the loaves, and the third dough ball (a bit smaller) was enough to make four medium-sized buns!

Use a Thermometer!

For testing the temperature of the water, I used my trusty digital prong Acu-Rite meat thermometer that I use for sticking in the breast meat of the Christmas turkey... it worked fine! Regarding proofing the bread (letting it rise), I also used the thermometer.

I set the oven to its lowest setting (mine was 150°F and then I cranked the door open to let in cooler air, and closed it when it dropped down to 85°F).

This is the temperature I chose to proof the bread at! All I did was drape an old clean (slightly dampened) dish towel over the bread tins. I realize that at 85°F, the towel wasn't going to set on fire so I felt OK using the oven!

I was able to close the oven door for both proofings so there were no drafts, and the temperature stayed at 85°F - just right! I am thrilled! I have baked this bread several times since, and each time it yields impressive bread! BUT -- and there's always a but! -- it never hangs around the house long enough to savor for more than a day or two! :-) What a fantastic way to save money though by baking your own!

Anita's Super-Easy Bread
use as Naan Bread or Pizza Dough

Introducing a super easy bread recipe from my buddy Anita, who lives in Scotland.

Anita ran a thriving business with her husband, James. Together they took to the roadsides of Britain, feeding hungry festival crowds with their belly-pleasin' hot baked potatoes, soups -- and sandwiches with their home-baked bread!

Anita and James kindly shared their super easy bread recipe with us, coming up!

Anita's Discovery

For years, Anita had been baking bread using her bread-making machine (like we all do!) but decided to just use it for making the dough only -- and to finish off the bread in a real oven. And you need to see the fantastic ovens that James creates! :-)

But then she made a discovery that totally changed the way she makes bread now!

She says it takes her "one trip out to the store" and for a few minutes each week she can put together enough dough to last her a week - and she stores the dough in her 'fridge! How great is that?

Her Naan bread goes great with curry (the Brits love their curry, kindly passed on to them by the Pakistanis), and Anita makes all kinds of pizzas, both vegetarian and 'regular'.

Her first loaf was 'artisan' in nature but didn't hang around the kitchen long enough to be 'appreciated' -- the aroma and butter won out... The next day she made flat bread stuffed with peppers and olives! Pizza came next... (heck, I'm moving to Scotland right now) and another loaf too followed by Naan bread the day after!

(Maybe we can get an airline discount if we all go over at once?)

How my BREAD and PIZZA turned out is coming up soon
.
OK, enough Talk, -- Here's Anita's Super Easy Bread Recipe!

Ingredients:

- 3 cups warm water
- 2 packets yeast
- 1-1/2 tablespoons sea salt
- 6-1/2 cups PLAIN flour (not bread or strong flour, just plain!)
- fine oatmeal for the pizza paddle

that's it!

We will need to get a plastic box, Anita uses one this size: 8" x 16" x 6" deep.

1) In the plastic box, add the warm water, yeast, and salt and mix in the flour. Use a wet hand or wooden spoon. The mixture should be quite wet - wet enough to actually flow into the corners of the box!

2) Let sit out at room temperature for two hours, to rise.

3) Take out what you need, and refrigerate the rest.

4) Grab a ball of dough, grapefruit-sized, to make a loaf. Don't over handle it, just shape it into a ball by pulling the sides under leaving a nice smooth top. Dust the paddle with the oatmeal and leave the loaf to rise. After 20 minutes, put the oven on to pre-heat and place a baking stone* and a water container in the oven. For the water container, an old pie-crust tin is good.

5) Don't put water in the container yet but make a couple of slashes across your dough (it helps to dust the bread first with flour -- great tip Anita!)

6) Preheat the oven to 475°F (Anita calls for 250°C so that's pretty close). I actually use 450°F when I'm making this, use what suits you best.

7) After 20 minutes of pre-heating, slide the loaf onto the stone. Pour a cup of water into the container, close the oven and patiently W-A-I-T.

8) Check in 20 to 25 minutes. Take the bread out and tap it, it should sound hollow when done. Anita says every oven is different, so do the tapping-test for hollowness.

9) Allow to cool completely (yeah, right). Spread with butter. Indulge. Enjoy.

* Anita uses four terra cotta tiles on a tray as her pizza stone!

Here's How Mine Turned Out...

I decided to try my hand at Anita's Bread and Pizza because a couple of days ago, Anita and James shared their bread recipe with me, and I decided to 'have a go' and make a loaf and a pie!

My husband brought home a pizza stone and a huge spatula combo kit from Target Stores. The spatula is made of stainless steel and it's a super heavy-duty spatula too!

The stone worked great, but I wish I could say the same for the spatula... even though I put on a good amount of ground-up oatmeal on it, I guess I let it sit on the slotted spatula too long, and it was a REAL pain to get it off, and on to the stone.

NOTE: See how the problem was fixed by reading how, coming up, regarding the spatula!

Nevertheless, it was SUPER tasty and quick and easy to make! Here's the dough, see pictures on the next page, just after mixing and then two hours later.

Anita asked me how the pizza making went, and I told her to have a look at the page you're reading now... and she kindly pointed out that I had not followed her directions!

Here's how to fix the spatula deal!

Anita uses non-stick parchment paper!!! I DO WISH I'd read that earlier... she cuts paper to fit the baking stone, puts the dough on it and lets it rest for 20 minutes THEN Anita bakes the EMPTY crust for about 2 to 3 minutes... then removed the parchment paper from underneath the crust. Remember to add the water here in the oven -- and I need to add be careful what 'container' you use as I shattered my Pyrex glass dish due to NOT having water in it and letting it heat up empty (sigh) so now I've got a tin-foil pie crust pan in there for the water!

NOW it's time to add the toppings after the crust has been baked... and I can't wait to report back to let you know how the spatula remedy worked this time! My hubby just walked by and said "that was your baseline pizza Susan!" :-) Also, Anita says to add the sauce first, then the cheeses, then the toppings! I'll get it right next time!

Look here! I did it right this time! Anita's Pizza Take-Two!

The photo below shows the rolled out dough for the pizza crust, then the spatula dusted with ground-up oatmeal, and then the crust with the edges rolled in to keep the sauce from rolling out!

Almost ready for the oven! Just need to add three cheeses: about 4 oz. of grated medium Cheddar, maybe 2 oz. of grated Parmesan, and about 3 oz. of Mozzarella. This is what I had on hand in the 'fridge.

Before the cheese though, was some homemade sauce, with some re-hydrated peppers, and mushrooms. Of course you can use fresh peppers and mushrooms too!

Into the oven it went... with a bit of a battle, but eventually I won but it wasn't a pretty sight.

And this is what it looked like 20 minutes later!

My husband had all that for his lunch -- he deserved it though, he'd been out mowing the grass. I ate the scrunched/messed up part from forcing it OFF the darned spatula... (I'm not brave enough to show that mess here!)

Anita's Bread... As it Turns Out IS Easy To Do!

Here's Anita's bread, and I wrote and asked her if I should have kneaded the bread at all? Answer: "No" -- so how easy is that? She said to just "mix it well, and then let it sit for two hours."

NOW EVEN I CAN DO THAT!

Here's the bread after its two hour wait, then floured lightly on top so I could score it. It's now ready for the oven! I decided to bake this first so that the pizza stone could get really warmed up.

Please note: I only used HALF the ingredients from Anita's recipe as it was my first time. So half the ingredients made this one loaf AND the pizza!

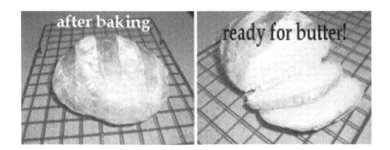

Pizza Take Two --
Success the Second Time Around...

This section was born for shame
of how my first pizza was PUSHED
OFF the pizza paddle/spatula...

I felt I had to make another one (such hardship there -- not!) but this time I followed Anita's instructions -- by using parchment paper and pre-cooking the pizza crust for a few minutes first ON the paper ON the stone in the oven!

I put the parchment paper on the spatula, cut it down to size and left about a one inch overlap of paper all around. I then placed the crust on it and shaped it so it wasn't hanging off the spatula/paddle!

There's the dough, directly above, ready for the oven, sat on the parchment paper. After the pre-bake in the oven, I brought it out and added my sauce, some sautéed onions; green, red, yellow peppers, and mushrooms.

I pricked the dough to stop bubbles from forming, then put it in the oven and baked it for 3 minutes. I then added the cheese, and then the olives, plus some of the veggies I'd saved aside to put purposely on top of the cheese.

TIP: next time I shall bake it for 5 minutes as my cheese ended up getting a little too brown for my liking because I was waiting for the crust to turn just the right shade of 'done'.

Into the oven it went for about 15 minutes - but see the TIP above about baking the crust first for probably 5 minutes. I forgot to mention earlier -- I've been using the oven at 450°F instead of 475°F. No real reason.

Tasty Herbed Bread
using "Anita Bread" as the base recipe

Here's two variations of Anita's Super Easy Bread again, and this time I've added plain old Italian Herbs to the dough recipe - nothing hard work or too fancy here, and the aroma this bread puts out while baking is mouthwatering... getting a grumbling tummy as I type this!

Herbed Anita Bread

Ingredients:

- 1-1/2 cups warm water

- 1 packet rapid-rise yeast

- 1-1/2 teaspoons sea salt

- 3-1/4 cups PLAIN flour (not bread or strong flour, just plain!)

- 3 tablespoons dried Italian herbs, more or less

that's it!

1) In a large mixing bowl put in the flour add the yeast packet, the salt and mix well. Add the herbs, mixing well - - use enough so that you can actually see the herbs! Then add the 120°F water. Use one hand to mix it all up, and use the back of a knife blade to scrape your hand clean! That tip passed down from my mom!

2) Let sit out at room temperature covered with an old clean tea towel, for one hour, to rise.

3) Knock down the risen dough, cover again, let sit another hour.

4) Turn the oven to 450°F and fill a shallow container with tap water (I use a small metal rectangular baking tin from the Dollar Store for this) and place it directly underneath your pizza stone, on the next rack down. Leave enough room above the pizza stone's rack so the dough can rise and not burn.

5) Shape the dough into an oblong loaf, pulling the sides down and under to create a nice smooth top. Put this dough on top of your pizza paddle with parchment paper directly on top of the paddle. This enables the dough to slide off the paddle, directly onto the stone in the oven.

6) Make a couple of slashes across your dough with a sharp knife and let sit on the parchment paper, on the paddle, while the oven heats up.

7) Bake for 5 minutes. Remove the parchment paper: Pull out the oven shelf, use an oven mitt and grab a corner of the parchment paper and use a small spatula to separate the bread from the paper, usually the paper will just slide right on out. Push the shelf back in and we're ready to finish baking!

8) Bake for 20 minutes. Take the bread out and tap it, it should sound hollow when done.

9) Allow to cool completely (yeah, right). Spread with butter. Indulge. Enjoy.

Herbed Bread with Garlic, Cheese, and Onion

using "Anita Bread" as the base recipe

Using the exact same ingredients as the Herbed Bread which makes one loaf, add these items to the dry mix before adding the water:

- 1 teaspoon garlic powder

- 2 tablespoons dehydrated onion, crushed

- 2 oz. shredded cheese of your choice

The dehydrated onion needs to be pretty fine, so get out your rolling pin, put the onion in a sandwich bag, and roll over it... or pop it in your blender/Magic Bullet™ . The water from the dough will re-hydrate the onion just fine!

I turned the oven down to 435°F about 3/4 the way through the baking time, as I didn't want the cheese to burn, but of course we want the bread to bake properly - so keep an eye on your bread for any signs of burning cheese! As an alternative, you could simply turn the oven off, about 5 minutes from the end, i.e. after 15 minutes.

And just another thought, if you find that the top is browning too fast, cover with aluminum foil – that way you can extend the baking time without the top burning!

Millet and Quinoa
suppliers of great nutrition!

Millet and Quinoa, but first... Millet

Millet has been around for centuries. It is widely grown around the world. It has many uses -- from nutrition to alcoholic beverages to porridge! Millet is very rich in B vitamins especially Niacin, B6 and Folic Acid, Potassium, Zinc and Calcium. The protein content (11% by weight) in millet is comparable to both flour and wheat.

As a kid I used to have a budgie (budgerigar/parakeet) named Mickey who used to have millet on the sprig pushed through his birdcage bars! He'd get those seeds everywhere! Later on in life, millet became an important ingredient in my diet. I add it to my soups and cauliflower mash. I also add millet (and quinoa) to my chicken chow dog food recipe.

I do rinse the millet in a fine sifter under running cool water before use although it doesn't have the bitterness of quinoa. I keep the millet and quinoa in separate plastic containers for daily/weekly use. When refills are needed, I scoop it out of the b-i-g plastic bags that it ships in. It's easier for me this way.

...and secondly, Quinoa

Just like millet, quinoa has also been around for centuries. Quinoa's protein content is very high - between 12% to 18%! It is a complete protein source - it contains the essential amino acids the body needs. Note: quinoa is pronounced 'keen-wah' It is a good source of fiber, and is high in Magnesium and Iron too.

The good news is that quinoa is gluten-free
so it makes it easier to digest for many folk.

I use quinoa in my cauliflower mash and in many soups to add an excellent source of protein. Quinoa (and millet) is also added to my chicken chow dog food recipe. Quinoa must be rinsed before use, as it has a bitter tasting coating. This is easily removed by rinsing under cool water in a fine sifter.

The sifter (or sieve) I use is from http://www.fantes.com and is a 10" Stainless Steel Extra Fine #17212. Around $20. They have a 9" sifter (#18889) which would be equally as good for about $4 less. It is an excellent product!

Better Than Bouillon
by Superior Touch

I just can't say enough good things about this "Better Than Bouillon" super product! I use it day in and day out! I discovered it years ago and I swear by it!

This photo above shows the "Better Than Bouillon" flavors I use on a regular basis: the big jars are ordered and shipped direct from Superior Touch (see ordering help below) and the smaller jars I buy when I need them at the local grocery store.

Sometimes you don't need or want extra jars of clam base, for instance, but you surely do need backup big jars of the chicken base and the vegetable base stocks.

You can order small jars too, either singly, or in 6-pks through the 'professional' side of Superior Touch but be aware that prices are cut in half if you go through 'professional' and then (this is important!:) 'FOODSERVICE'. Only 16oz containers are available from their 'Foodservice' section at half price. You end up getting twice as much for your money this way!

They have a long shelf-life, so don't worry about them expiring too soon. When you have opened a container, keep it in the refrigerator where it'll last for months too!

The flavors are delicious -- and they have organic varieties too along with vegetarian, reduced sodium, and kosher based stocks!

Superior Touch also sell gravies and crock-pot seasoning mixes. Visit them at http://www.superiortouch.com

Consider this a 'both thumbs up' endorsement!

Don't forget to check out our recipes where many of them use this super-tasty bouillon.

61
FOOD GLORIOUS FOOD!

No Asking for More --
We Must Work with What We Have

Many of us know the 'food glorious food' story of orphan-boy Oliver, asking for "more" at the dinner table... but our situation today is a far cry from Oliver's plight! I open my fridge/freezer doors, there's food.

Open my pantry door, there it sits.
Look on my kitchen counter top...
I can't get away from it!

This may all be 'fine and dandy' but are YOU prepared in the event of a food shortage?

Is There Enough to Go Around?
Just looking around at passersby, the average person to me isn't built like there's 'not enough food to go around'... the grocery stores are chock-full of it; it's in every restaurant; it's eaten at every birthday, holiday, and celebration party!

There's food to eat when we're sad - and when we're happy. Food Glorious Food. As a nation, we are obsessed with it -- we eat too much of it -- just look at the diet industry spawned by overeating!

So it's no surprise really to find that people are not panicking over a 'lack of food', or lack of anything, for that matter.

That's good. I'm not here to make people panic. I just want people to be prepared, just in case that rainy day does come along and there's not enough food glorious food on our dining tables.

If you are prepared (have some put away or are growing your own) then you've nothing to fear... and you'll be able to help your other family members and maybe your neighbors!

Japan's Rainy Day
We have unrest in the Middle East; tragic earthquakes and nuclear accidents in Japan -- and who knows how it's all going to end up?

'Quakes in California and Manhattan? Perhaps, or even Tennessee, Kentucky, Indiana - along the New Madrid fault line?...

Nobody knows what is going to happen or when it's going to happen. But I know one thing, I certainly want to be prepared for it if it does happen. There's nothing worse than feeling out of the loop and then kicking yourself later for not having prepared when you had the chance. So keep an eye on Fox News!

US Dollar Meltdown?

Then there's the likely meltdown of the US dollar. Due to Japan's ongoing catastrophe, Japan won't have any 'spare money' to buy our debt (to help prop up the US dollar); their money will be better used to rebuild their infrastructure. That only leaves China who carries lots of US debt on their books already.

What happens when China no longer wants our debt? The US dollar will fail. There's no-one left to buy our debt! The US government keeps monetizing the US debt (as in printing more dollars) and that creates inflation.

Too much debt monetizing leads to hyperinflation. Look at the two year period of 1921 - 1923 in Weimar Republic (Germany). Their hyperinflation wasn't the worst in history, it was officially beaten by Hungary and Zimbabwe.

Don't panic! History shows that fiat currencies usually 'only' have a lifespan of '30 to 40 years', so if history is right, then the US dollar is ready for a collapse.

And if the dollar does collapse, then that'll be one heck of a challenge for all of America and the world. Yes, a new monetary system will be put in place, and in my humble opinion, there'll be general unrest and outrage for a while as to why 'every-day people on the street' did NOT know what was going on, or at least fully understand the implications of 'fiat currency'... so I'm saying be prepared by having more food glorious food put away by dehydrating what you have, right now!

Learn more about fiat currencies by visiting Amazon.com's book section. It's called Rich Dad's Advisors: Guide to Investing in Gold and Silver, Protect Your Financial Future. Look for Mike Maloney too, he's great!

The hardest hit will be the poor and middle class who don't have enough money put away for the rainy day -- those of us who are living paycheck to paycheck. All this is compounded by insidious inflation - you can't get ahead, no matter how hard you try!

Buy Stuff with Real Money – Gold and Silver

If the dollar fails,
what will you buy food with?
Real money.

When the dust settles,
a new currency will be put in place.

So, to continue: We can prepare now by perhaps becoming a little less reliant on the big grocery store chains and start to become a little more self-sufficient by growing our own vegetables and fruits.

Sock away some bags of flour, quinoa, millet, lentils, peas, beans - now. These are all great food staples. It's learning what to do with 'em that counts! It's back to basics! We have quite a few easy tasty recipes using the above ingredients listed earlier on in this book.

Inflated (Unaffordable) Food Prices

What happens when people can't afford
to buy food at today's rapidly inflating prices?
What happens when it rots in the stores, or worse, just plain runs out? Are you prepared for that scenario?

If you've been prudent, you'll at least have some canned meats and canned fish (tuna, salmon, crab, and mackerel) items for protein put away.

Some packs of dried milk, maybe powdered eggs, bottled water. If you've been REALLY GOOD(!) and are very much prepared, then you'll have lots of dehydrated vegetables and fruits already packed away!

62
WHY
DEHYDRATE FOOD?

The Time is NOW to Get Prepared... by dehydrating food for the long-term

"Why Dehydrate Food?" you may be asking yourself –

Things Are About To Change...

You may have noticed that there's not much talk about hyper-inflation in the mainstream news, let alone talk about 'regular' inflation... because it's a very scary situation.

Millions of Americans may be faced with having little or NO food to put on their dining tables, and it's pretty much unimaginable that this "land of plenty" could possibly be anything but.

Now's the time to start dehydrating foods
while food is readily available,
at somewhat reasonable prices,
before inflation hits big-time.

The sobering reality is: inflation is caused by the Fed's excessive printing of money, in the form of Quantitative Easing, be it in actual note printing, or the digitized version... and many people do not realize that this excess 'money' being printed actually dilutes the spending power of the 'money' that is actually 'out there' in circulation already.

Yes, But Look What our House is Worth Now!

Imagine this: I used to think that oooh, look, our house is now worth $25,000 more than it was three years ago! Happy days! -- WRONG! -- Why?

The actual value of our home didn't change at all... simply the price of it did... and the fact that now, three years later, it simply needs an extra $25,000 to buy it because the VALUE of the dollar has dropped, thereby needing more dollars to purchase our home! (Note: this increased-home-price scenario was in the 'good old days' of 2003-2005!!!)

The house price seemed to 'have gone up' when in fact, it's due to the dollar's demise and excess money in circulation. Inflation has diluted the buying power of the dollar. The simple fact is that it takes MORE dollars now to buy it. Unfortunately now we're in the downward cycle in the housing market which generally runs in seven year cycles.

Let us clarify something here, money, as we're used to thinking of as our paper notes which we stuff in our wallets, is NOT money — it is 'currency' with a promise that its worth is backed by the full faith and credit of the United States Government.

That's another scary point. When the rest of the world loses 'faith' in the USA, what could happen?

Paper Money is "Currency"

And what happens if the 'credit rating' of the US slips again? Not to mention the sixteen TRILLION dollar debt...

You guessed it -- the dollar's value falls even more, which you may have been witnessing these past few years. And then inflation sets in and prices rise in other areas. Areas such as the commodities: oil, food; you know - the stuff we need for everyday living!

So, What IS Real Money?

Think back to the good old days – well not that far back – but back to the 1970s. The dollar used to be backed by gold, in other words, you could exchange your paper dollars for the equivalent amount of gold… until President Nixon took us off the 'gold standard'. The only 'real money' is Gold or Silver, i.e. precious metals.

When Mr. Nixon un-pegged the dollar from gold, it meant that the dollar was in fact backed by nothing but the 'good faith and credit of the United States Government' as mentioned above.

At that time, the dollar was worth a dollar, until inflation hit…

But Wait, it Gets Worse -- In fact, this is the very first time in HISTORY that all of the major world currencies are pegged to the US Dollar, so when the dollar fails, so follows all the other major countries' currencies that are pegged to the US dollar! Another name for these currencies is 'fiat' currencies. Fiat actually is Latin meaning "let it be done"… and that simply equates to "any money declared by a government to be legal tender". Just thought you'd like to know! And that's where buying precious metals comes into play.

– THE END –
THANK YOU FOR READING and PURCHASING THIS BOOK
We hope you got a lot of useful information to aid you
in your food dehydrating foray!

ABOUT THE AUTHOR

Susan Gast lives in Sunny Florida
with her ever-patient and ever-encouraging
husband, an adopted Miniature Pinscher
(who runs the house), lots of raw food,
two food dehydrators, one vacuum-sealing machine,
a couple of computers,
and reams of scribbled notes
on the backside of previously printed paper!

~*~

Now that you've come to the end of this book, please leave me a review over at Amazon.com... Here's the link:

http://www.amazon.com/dp/B0093ZGX3Q

Leaving a review really helps others decide whether or not to buy this book. *Your opinion matters,* and helps me to address any problems too. Thank You!

Cheers, Susan

Made in the USA
Lexington, KY
03 August 2015